EAST VILLAGE
DES MOINES

EAST VILLAGE
DES MOINES
· A BRIEF HISTORY ·

HOPE MITCHELL

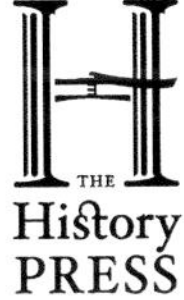

Published by The History Press
Charleston, SC
www.historypress.net

Front cover: Wikimedia Commons, Iqkotze.

First published 2016

Manufactured in the United States

ISBN 978.1.46711.962.7

Library of Congress Control Number: 2016944044

Contents

Acknowledgements

This book would not have been possible without the unwavering support of my wonderful husband, family and friends, all of whom listened to countless hours of rambling about fun facts concerning the East Village and the history of Des Moines (fun fact: the first sheriff of Des Moines shares his name with my father), put up with the constant presence of various piles of books and boxes of notes that at times took over our home, assisted me in finding my words when I was sure I had lost them and mostly never doubted that I would someday finish this book.

Secondly, I owe a tremendous thank-you to John Zeller, Sarah Oltrogge and Jim Jacobsen for generously sharing their time and insight into this wonderful neighborhood with me.

Finally, thank you to Becki Plunkett at the State Historical Society of Iowa (SHSI-DM) and Catherine Bierling with the Des Moines Public Library (DMPL) for their assistance in locating photos that portray the growth and development of the East Village.

INTRODUCTION

It was a sweltering Iowa summer day in August 1929 as Jerry Gardineer made his way out to his front porch. He had come outside to read the paper while he waited for the reporter from the *Des Moines Tribune-Capital*. Apparently, the young man was curious about the history of the old red-light district on East Court Avenue, and since Jerry had made his home in the eastern half of Des Moines, he was just the man for the job. He had come outside hoping to catch a nice breeze, but no such luck. Instead, Jerry sat there fanning himself with the newspaper and looked out over the neighborhood that had been his home for so many years.

What had once been a loud, rough-and-tumble neighborhood of Des Moines was now consumed by peace and quiet. The only thing that ever disturbed his peace was the occasional clatter of a motorcar as it rumbled down the street or the hum of some legitimate business. While Jerry had to admit that since he had gotten older he tended to appreciate the quiet, he still sometimes missed the hustle and bustle of the old neighborhood. Jerry could not help but smile when thinking about the scrapes they got into. This was the sort of place where brawls broke out every night, but no one bothered to call the police. He chuckled as he remembered one night when the police had ventured down to Fifth Street, the most dangerous of all the streets in the neighborhood, to arrest a big burly Irish butcher for causing a fight. When they arrived, the giant Irishman had simply plucked two policemen off their wagon and ridden off with it for himself![1]

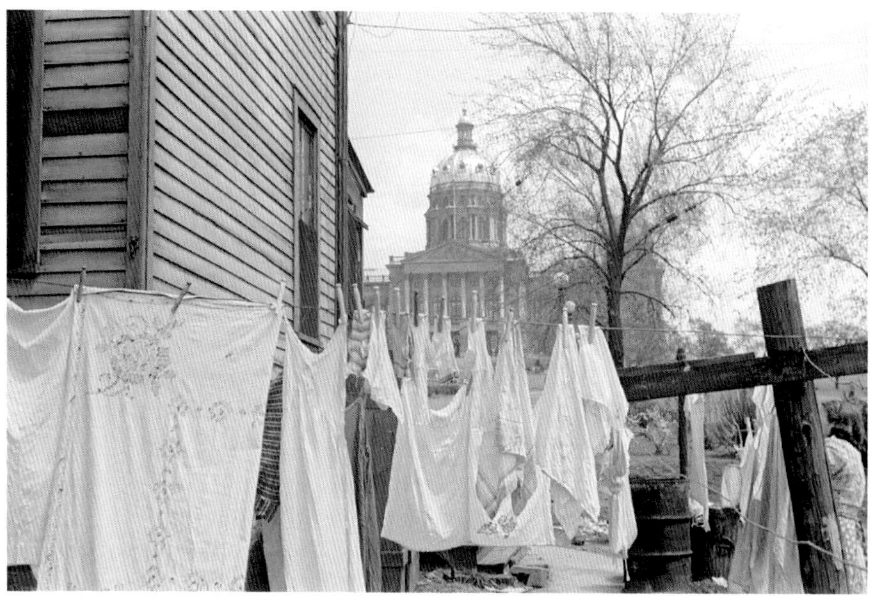

An image showcasing the contrast of the neighborhood surrounding the state capitol. *Library of Congress, Prints & Photographs Division, FSA/OWI Collection LC-USF33-T01-001868.*

Ironically, just a few blocks away from the vice and crime of Jerry's longtime neighborhood along East Court Avenue was the business district. Centered on East Locust Avenue, some of the city's most prominent business owners made their mark on the city; from his porch, Jerry could see the east side's two lonely skyscrapers, the Capital City State Bank and the Teachout Building, towering over the busy and bustling neighborhood. Looking over all of this was the shining golden-domed state capitol up on the hill. Beyond the capitol was the state fairgrounds, which brought together the best of the state's agricultural offerings in the heart of downtown.

While much has certainly changed throughout the neighborhood, in some ways things are still very much the same. There may no longer be a thriving red-light district and the neighborhood may have adopted a new name, but the character and culture of the East Village have held true. The neighborhood might once have been a series of contradicting parties, between the capitol on the hill, the agriculturally based state fair just east of the state capitol and the hardworking legitimate business owners located just blocks away from one of the largest centers of vice and crime. Today, we still see some of those same contradictions, pairing cutting-edge business ventures with historically significant architecture, but instead of warring with one another, the result is a vibrant, diverse and progressive neighborhood full of passionate innovators intent on preserving the heritage of their neighborhood. The East Village, which spans from the state capitol grounds to the river, is framed by I-235 to the north and Court Avenue to the south. This book will explore the events and parties that ultimately helped to shape the landscape and culture of what would become the East Village.

Chapter 1

Early East Des Moines

On the morning of May 9, 1843, a lone steamer named the *Ione* chugged slowly up the Des Moines River in search of the ideal site for a new fort. Captain James Allen, the leader of this expedition, was soon on deck shouting orders to his small detachment of troops. Captain Allen was an experienced and determined officer and was widely regarded as a man in possession of sound judgment and excellent military talents. The Sioux Indians who inhabited the area were a constant threat in the newly acquired territory. Government officials worried that the cunning and merciless Sioux would easily overwhelm any incoming settlers and therefore sent in Captain Allen and his detachment of soldiers to establish a fort in the new territory as a measure of protection.[2]

As the *Ione* continued to chug upriver, the men came to a point that was then known as the Raccoon Forks, where the Des Moines River intersected with the Raccoon River. Sailing just a little farther north, the ship laid anchor on the western bank of the Des Moines River at the foot of what would someday become Court Avenue. The men quickly began trekking through the muddy riverbank, unloading what little baggage they had carried north with them. More importantly, they also began unloading the military stores and materials that would help them assemble their new fort. Allen instructed the men to begin work building the fort while he headed back downriver with the steamer, promising to return in a month or so with more troops to assist in constructing and manning the fort.[3]

A month or so later, Captain Allen kept his promise and returned with the remaining troops, and they quickly began work on building the barracks necessary to house all the men. In Captain Allen's absence, the men had set up camp where Court Avenue now sits, and while life along the river was not always comfortable, the men managed to stay in good spirits. The work was certainly long and hard, but the men kept up a jovial atmosphere around the campsite. Every morning, a beating drum and a loud calling of a bugle echoed from the surrounding hills, signaling the start of the day. The men would groggily rub the sleep from their eyes; they were maybe even invigorated by the balmy healthful air of the countryside, which had yet to feel "the despoiling hand of civilization." Their days were filled with hard labor building the fort and camaraderie, while at night the sound of their songs and laughter mingled with the constant lull of the rushing river. The fort they constructed extended north along the Des Moines River, with a second portion running parallel to the west, forming a triangular structure that opened out to the north and west and looked over to the eastern bank of the river.[4]

In total, they numbered approximately one hundred men. Their party was made up of two companies: one infantry, commanded by Lieutenants King and Potter, and one cavalry, commanded by Lieutenant Greer. With all these able-bodied men, the fort grew quickly from the initial structure. The men quickly set to work constructing several long one-story log structures in what would eventually become the business district of the city. All in all, the soldiers constructed approximately twenty buildings that served as barracks to keep the men warm through the long Iowa winters and stables to house their horses.[5]

It was no mistake that Allen and his crew had chosen to build their fort on the western bank of the Des Moines River. As historian H.B. Turrill recounted in his 1857 history of the city:

> *The eastern side is not so favorable, by nature for a town site, as the western. The space between the rivers and the adjacent hills is narrower, and a considerable portion of the valley is low and subject, in times of high water, to be partly overflowed. There is a level stretch of ground near the bluffs that is higher, and were it sufficiently extensive would constitute an admirable site for a town.*[6]

While all this early development occurred on the west side of the Des Moines River, the construction ultimately drew settlers to the area surrounding the new fort, and in spite of the unfortunate topography on the eastern bank, many incoming settlers made their home in what would ultimately become East Des Moines.

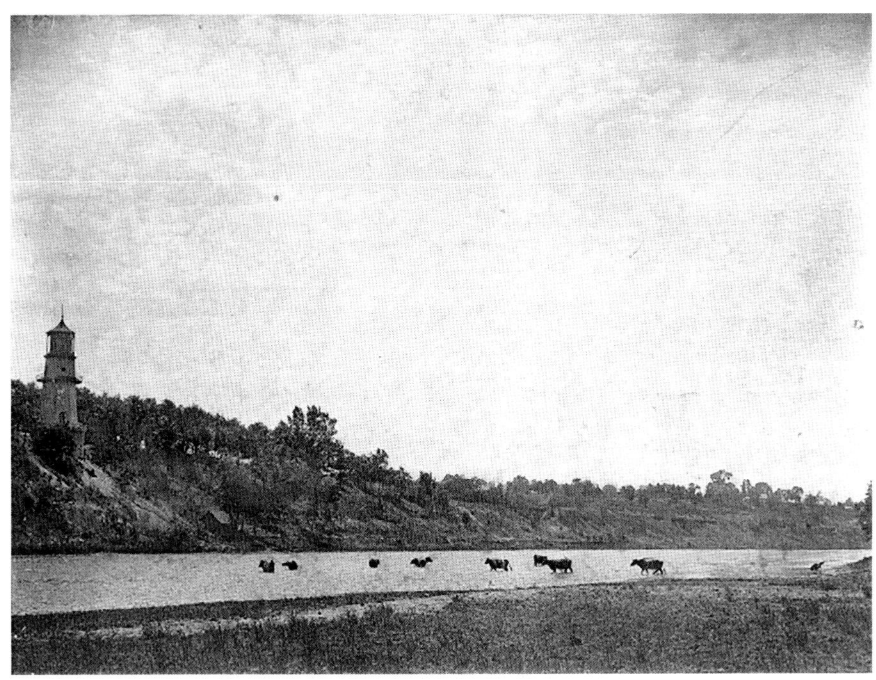

A photo of the eastern bank of the Des Moines River; note the steep grade of the riverbank. *DMPL available through a CC-BY License.*

Prior to the construction of the fort, a treaty had been signed with the Native Americans in the area that agreed to keep white settlers off the land until October 1845. Unfortunately, the rumors of the fertile land in the Iowa territory proved too tempting for some, and a few settlers did manage to gain permission from the government agents and were able to settle near the newly constructed fort at the junction of the Des Moines and Raccoon Rivers. Many of the settlers brought their families along with them, and soon enough, the fort that had once housed soldiers and their horses began to resemble a quaint little village. Often, these families were able to gain access to the restricted lands because of the services they promised to provide for the residents of the fort. John and W.A. Scott, whose farm was located on the eastern bank of the river approximately where Grand Avenue runs today, not only provided agricultural provisions to the fort but also supplied a ferry service across the river for residents in and surrounding the fort. Like the Scott brothers, farmers William Lamb and Alexander Turner were contracted to supply the fort with hay, grain and various other agricultural products. Likewise, Charles Weatherford served as blacksmith and J.M.

Thrift and James Drake worked as gunsmiths for the Native Americans in the area.[7]

With the construction of the fort on the west side of the Des Moines River, many of the incoming settlers took up residence on the east side of the river, making them the original east siders. The inaugural building in what would become East Des Moines was the Agency House; the agency was an extension of the fort and housed a trading post operated by Phelps and Company. After the fort was abandoned a few years later, the Agency House and its surrounding property were acquired by prominent East Des Moines resident Dr. T.K. Brooks. Of all the new settlers to arrive at the fort on the Des Moines River, the Ewing brothers, Washington George, or W.G., and George Washington, known as G.W., were potentially the most noteworthy additions to the newly founded fort. The uniquely named brothers were known as "men of rare energy, shrewdness, and courage."[8] The Ewing brothers were Indian traders and set up shop on the east side of the Des Moines River. Aside from operating their trading business, the brothers were credited with constructing the first "regular dwelling house" in Polk County. Like the other original structures surrounding the fort, the house was a "rude log cabin." Along with the Ewing brothers, several others made their home on the east side of the Des Moines River. The American Fur Company was one such business to set up shop. Just to the east of the American Fur Company, Native American agent Major Beach and interpreter Joseph Smart took up residence, since proximity to the Native Americans and traders was clearly advantageous for both parties. Beach and Smart's dwelling was near several smith shops operated by the Sturdevant and Drake families, who provided smithing services for the Sac and Fox tribes in the area.[9]

Aside from the soldiers' arrival on the banks of the Des Moines River on May 9, 1843, the second most exciting day in the written memory of this city might be October 11, 1845. This was the day when the treaty with the neighboring Native American tribes ended and the settlers who had made their way to the fort were finally able to officially stake their claims on up to 320 acres of land. In fact, this night was so highly anticipated that in the weeks leading up to the end of the treaty, the current residents who had gained permission to make their homes around the fort by providing for the soldiers had already begun making arrangements with one another and verbally reserving the most valuable tracts of land for themselves. Some settlers had even gone so far as to actually measure and stake out their claims using temporary markers so as to make it easier to find and quickly mark out their plots of land when the treaty ended at midnight on October 11. Of

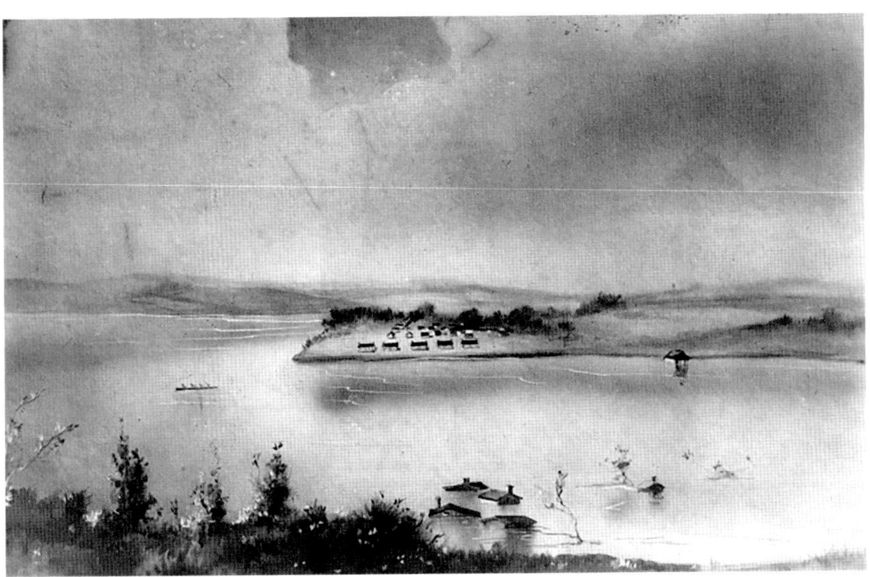

A view of the original Fort Des Moines from the eastern bank. *DMPL available through a CC-BY License.*

course, these actions carried no real weight, but they did demonstrate the seriousness of staking claims and worked to heighten anticipation for the end of the treaty.[10]

As the clock approached midnight on the eve of October 10, 1845, the residents of Fort Des Moines anxiously waited just outside the square-mile perimeter that had been plotted around and reserved for the fort for the signal to begin plotting their claims. Soldiers from the fort were stationed throughout the eager masses with orders to assist settlers by measuring out claims. As the clock struck twelve, a shot sounded from the Agency House on the hill of the eastern bank of the Des Moines River to announce the end of the treaty. In return, shots rang out for miles around in celebration as hundreds of settlers rushed the land to claim their future homes and fortunes. With the moon sinking slowly in the west casting a dim light over the fields, it was possible to watch the bobbing torches of settlers move across the field from the Agency House.[11]

While the land surrounding the fort on both sides of the river was busy being claimed and developed by the incoming rush of settlers, the fort itself was experiencing the opposite effect. Shortly after the end of the treaty in October, some of the troops were removed from the fort and relocated elsewhere. The remaining troops continued on at the fort until June 1846, when they were also removed. After the removal of the troops, Congress gave the 160 acres belonging to the fort, as well as all the structures on the land, to the recently formed Polk County. Ultimately, the removal of the troops worked to the benefit of the continued development of the community growing around the fort. As the soldiers evacuated the fort, the influx of newly arrived citizens and the new community that developed as a result used the former fort's barracks to house various public offices for the county.[12]

As the new county continued to grow and develop, the citizens who had made their homes there continued to experience many firsts. The first election in Polk County took place on the first Monday of April 1846 for the purpose of electing county officers. Three polling centers were made available throughout the county: Thomas Mitchell's place in Camp Creek precinct, J.D. Parmelee's home located near Allen's Mill and finally a polling center was placed in a former dragoon house, known as the Point, in the old fort. The first election garnered a total of 175 votes, with 42 votes cast at Mitchell's home, 63 at the location near Allen's Mill and 70 votes cast at the fort. This was an impressive turnout for the very first election, as the total number of inhabitants in the county in 1846 was between two and three hundred. Prominent citizens G.B. Clark, W.H. Meacham and T.K. Brooks oversaw the three polling sites. This was quite an honor, considering that both Meacham and Brooks were east siders. Brooks had taken over the Agency House, and Meacham ran a horse-powered sawmill on the eastern bank of the river. Among the county officers elected, both Clark and Meacham were chosen as county officials, with Meacham serving as one of the three appointed county commissioners and Clark elected to the post of county assessor. They were joined by Thomas Mitchell, who was elected as the first sheriff of Polk County; James Phillips as coroner; and Addison Michael as the county collector. These newly elected officials soon made their office in a log cabin on the western bank of the river belonging to the former fort. Even though the citizens of East Des Moines had certainly played a prominent role in the fort's first official election, it is worth noting that just two months later in June 1846, when the citizens of Fort Des Moines drafted their first town charter, those residing on the eastern bank of the river were excluded.[13]

While the newly elected county officials made their home in the former fort, ready to set about maintaining order across the county, a more developed justice system also made its way to Polk County. The newly formed county fell under the jurisdiction of the Honorable Joseph Williams. On April 2, 1846, Williams took up office near the newly appointed county officials in another log shanty once belonging to the former fort. Williams quickly set about appointing a band of grand jurors composed of twenty-two men. While these men were a self-described "uncouth and barbarous looking set," they were nonetheless a group of good men who were determined to maintain peace within the county. Judge Williams, who had also been appointed to keep the peace within the county, joked that these men had "clean hearts under dirty shirts; and that in a new county every allowance was to be made for their personal attire and appearance." Thankfully, their job was quite simple, as there was very little crime within the newly established Polk County.[14]

Starting on July 15, 1846, a notice ran for the following three weeks in the *Iowa Capital Reporter* in Iowa City, the *Burlington Hawkeye* and the *Iowa Democrat* in Keosauqua announcing the sale of lots in Fort Des Moines. Many of the lots advertised were along what would become prime real estate in the coming years. For example, lots along Court Avenue were sold for as little as $18, and just ten years later, it was estimated that those same lots had skyrocketed in value up to $5,000. With the sale of these lots, buildings began to rapidly spring up around the Des Moines River. This continued development of the city was fueled by all the natural resources along the Des Moines and Raccoon Rivers. The heavy timber that lined the rivers provided all the necessary lumber, while the coal and stone beds that lay in the nearby hills also provided opportunity for future development and industry.[15]

The sale of these plots took place in Iowa City in 1848, but the purchasing of this land was not nearly as easy as one would expect. The settlers had chosen and held their claims on the basis of pre-emption, which enabled settlers to hold one hundred acres. This land would eventually be surveyed and brought to market, but the settler would have the right to purchase his pre-empted land at the minimum rate of $1.25 per acre. This was an incredible bargain, given that the land around the junction of the Des Moines and Raccoon Rivers was covered in valuable timber, rich prairie and rich deposits of stone, coal and other valuable materials. These tracts of land were valued at anywhere from $2.00 to $12.00 an acre. Even though the United States government held ownership of the land until the time of the sale, those who had claimed these tracts of land were considered to be quite fortunate.[16]

Unfortunately, it was common knowledge that speculators roamed the land and had taken note of the most valuable acres to be found around Fort Des Moines. Even though settlers had already claimed these tracts of land, the speculators were willing to pay a higher price for these portions of land when they came to market. The settlers who had claimed this land and spent the last several years taming and managing it were obviously enraged by the thought that their hard-earned land might be stolen right from under them. The fear of speculators caused the settlers to view any new passersby in the area with extreme distrust, worrying that their intent might be to steal their claimed land. In order to ensure that these speculators did not steal their land, the settlers around the former fort appointed R.L. Tidrick to act as their agent at the land sales. Along with a corps of armed men instructed to "use any means however forcible and violent," Tidrick was to make his way to Iowa City carrying all the money allotted for the purchasing of land around Fort Des Moines in order to protect "the rights of the settlers in [that] vicinity from any injury on the part of other bidders, and to prevent those claims from being sold which the holders wished to pay for." Thankfully, Tidrick safely made his way to Iowa City and successfully purchased all the claimed land.[17]

In 1852, a U.S. Land Office was established in Fort Des Moines in order to continue facilitating land sales in the area. As had been the case in 1848, there were those individuals who sought to use their buying power to purchase land right out from under those who had rightfully claimed it. Such was the case with a man named Bates. Many had heard Bates boasting around town that no one "should deter him from buying whatever land he chose. He had some money…and as far as it would go, he meant to invest it in claims, just to teach the settlers that [they] could not scare everybody from doing what was allowed by law." Of course, when the day of purchase arrived, Bates was waiting outside the land office, ready to make his bid. As soon as he opened his mouth, though, Bates found himself surrounded by a group of men who kindly escorted him down to the steamboat landing on the Des Moines River, where they held him until he swore he would not attempt to purchase any tract of land that was not rightfully his.[18]

While the citizens on the eastern bank of the river had successfully protected their claims, in 1851 they faced a new kind of challenge. In May of that year, the *Iowa Star* reported:

> *Neither the memory of the oldest inhabitants along the banks of the Des Moines river, nor the memory of natives, who resided here before it was settled by the white, nor an accounts from the Indians, furnishes any evidence of such a flood having occurred here in all past time. The 'Coon and the Des Moines are higher by several feet* [than] *they were in the spring of 1849, which was the greatest rise of water ever known here up to that time.*[19]

From the earliest days, residents around the former fort had noted that the eastern banks of the Des Moines River had a tendency to flood. Such was the case in 1851 when the city saw record floods that "overflowed entirely up to the second bank, and the swollen waters covered all the bottoms and swept around the hill." The floodwaters were so strong that they "swept away or hopelessly wrecked" the few buildings located near the base of the river. Amid all the destruction of the flooding, some east siders did try to make the best of a bad situation. Prominent east side business owner Isaac Brandt, who operated a store on East Locust, resorted to using a steamboat to receive his supplies.[20]

The ease with which the eastern bank of the Des Moines River flooded made it difficult to formally plat out the land, but that did not stop east siders from laying out their half of the city. Aside from the citizens who resided closer to the bank, two other townships had formed nearby. John Saylor formed a town aptly called Saylorville just north of what would become East Des Moines. Notable east sider Dr. T.K. Brooks even attempted to form his own town just a few miles east of the river. Brooks's town went by several names, including Brooklyn, Brooks and Brook's Church, before it was finally reabsorbed into Des Moines. W.A. Scott and John S. Dean made one of the first formal efforts to plat out the eastern bank in

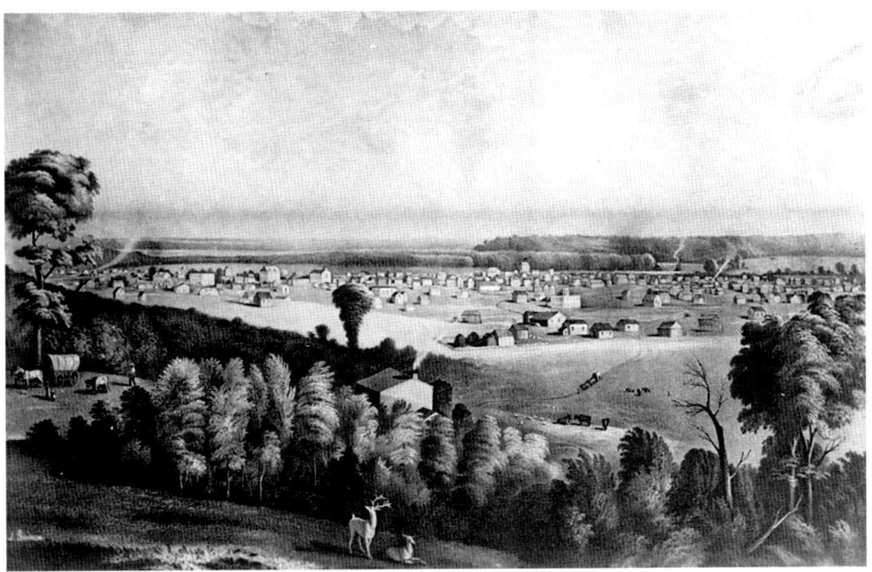

An 1856 scene, looking southeast from Fifteenth and Woodland. *DMPL available through a CC-BY License.*

1849, platting out the highly flooded area just west of Fourth Street and south of Locust. After the east side was finally incorporated into Greater Fort Des Moines in 1853, some of the larger landowners on the east side spearheaded a more concerted effort to formally plot out the remaining land on the eastern bank, helping to begin to shape the east side as we know it today.[21]

With their claims purchased and their half of the town formally platted, the early east siders could finally settle into their new homes, secure in the comfort that the land was truly theirs. While it had been only ten years since Captain James Allen laid anchor on the banks of the Des Moines River, so much had changed in that short amount of time. What had once been rough and wild lands untouched by settlers was now an incorporated town dotted by the early signs of industry. Where there had once been bushes of hazel lining the banks of the river, those bushes had now been cleared away to make room for the trading houses and mills. Along the rolling hills that surrounded the rivers, one could now see houses and fences going up, delineating one man's land from another's. The Sac and Fox, who had played a large role in the early history of the citizens of Fort Des Moines, now hardly made their way into the historical recounting of this newfound city. These citizens of Fort Des Moines had even progressed so far as to enact their own elections and incorporate themselves into the judicial system. In fact, Fort Des Moines had grown to the point where many were now eyeing the growing city as a potential candidate to house the state capitol.

Chapter 2

Constructing the Capitol

The beginnings of Iowa's first capitol started with a wooden stake that read "Seat of Government City of Iowa," hammered into the ground of Iowa City on May 4, 1839. Federal delegate W.W. Chapman had acquired the plot of land, and a $20,000 appropriation was set aside for the construction of a public capitol building. By the end of the year, architectural plans for what would become the old stone capitol had been submitted to the assembly for approval. Ultimately, the assembly signed off on the designs, and Iowa's first capitol was up and running by 1842. While not fully completed, legislators were eager to move in and begin working in their first official capitol, so the Iowa Territory's fifth legislative assembly was the first to meet in the stone capitol building of Iowa City.[22]

For sixteen years, Iowa's legislators made their home in Iowa City. During this time, the old stone capitol in Iowa City housed fourteen sessions of the legislature and saw three meetings of the state constitutional convention. Initially, when Iowa was a new territory, Iowa City had made perfect sense as the location for the state capital. With a majority of the first towns in the territory being located along the Mississippi River, Iowa City's eastern location was convenient for a majority of citizens. But as Iowa continued to grow, more and more people began to move westward and away from the current capital. Just over a decade after the old stone capitol was constructed in Iowa City, Iowa's population had tripled, growing from 116,454 to 326,5000 residents. These new settlers were making their way to the center and western edges of the state. This westward movement

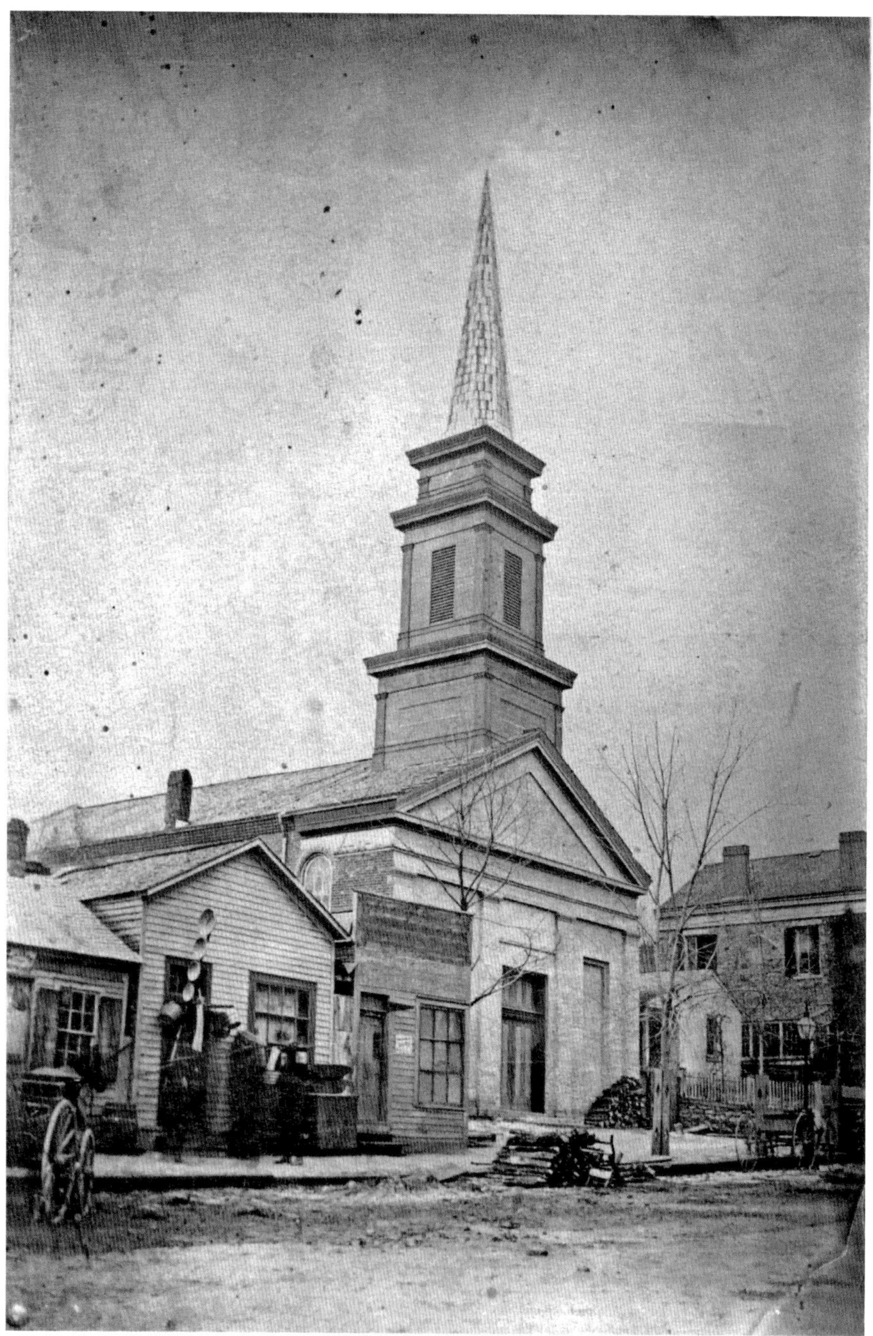

Prior to constructing the first capitol building, delegates met in the Zion Methodist Church in Burlington. *SHSI-DM: 5000.212.*

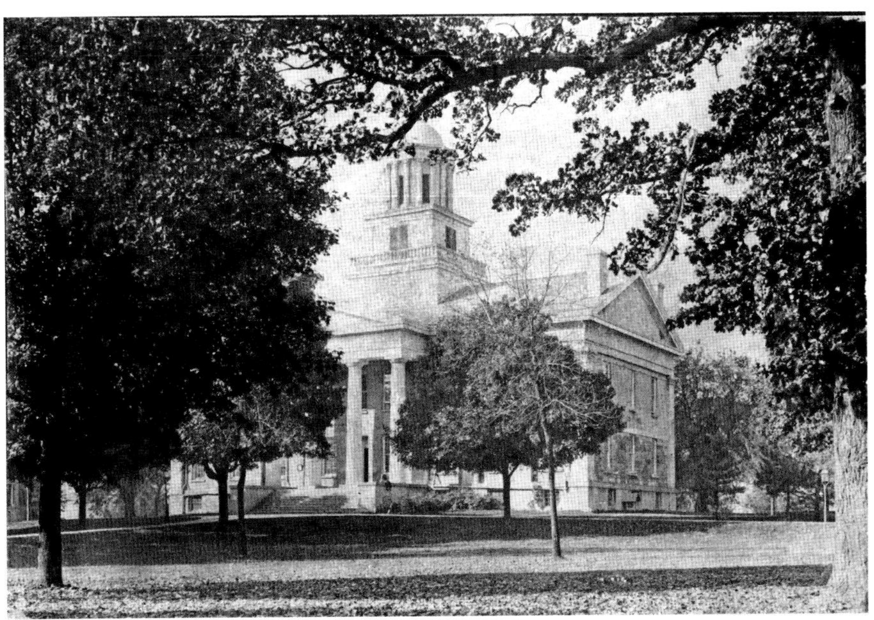

The old stone capitol in Iowa City. *SHSI-DM: 14775.*

meant that the early settlements along the Mississippi River were no longer the only significant centers of population in the state, and this westward movement likely meant an upcoming shift of power within the new state.[23]

All of this westward movement meant that Iowa's residents began pondering the possibility of a more centrally located state capital that could better serve the growing population. The first real action toward moving the capital came in February 1847, when Governor Briggs approved a bill passed by the general assembly that intended "to provide for the location of the Seat of Government of the State of Iowa, and for the selection of land granted by Congress to aid in erecting public buildings." The one stipulation of this bill was that the new capital must be placed as close to the geographic center of the state as possible. Not surprisingly, there was talk of moving the state's capital to the more centrally located Fort Des Moines. While Fort Des Moines was still relatively young, the general assembly had taken note of how well and how rapidly the new fort was developing. With the rush of new residents and the sudden influx of wealth these settlers inevitably brought with them, the city around the former fort had become a site of great commercial importance. This change was so obvious to the residents of Iowa that by 1846, Fort Des Moines was named the county seat of Polk County, and by 1853, Fort Des Moines was incorporated by the state legislature.[24]

While those residents of the current capital in Iowa City were in favor of maintaining the status quo, other residents of the state were interested in seeing the capital migrate toward the center of the state. By 1850, petitions had begun pouring into the general assembly outlining a long list of potential towns that would be interested in hosting the new capital. For a time, the assembly seriously considered moving the capital to Jasper County, but it was determined that the location would be too rural, and it was rejected by the assembly. While many towns vied for this position, many believed that Fort Des Moines would serve as an ideal location. These hopes came to fruition in 1854, when a bill was introduced and passed through the state legislature in favor of moving the capital to the fort along the Des Moines River. For obvious reasons, this bill was strongly opposed by members of the legislature who resided in the eastern portion of the state, but their complaints ultimately fell on deaf ears. This bill did make one concession to the residents of the eastern portion of the state: it stated that the capitol would remain in Iowa City for two more years.[25]

During this time, the statesmen from Johnson County and other surrounding counties began plotting the ways in which they could repeal the bill to relocate the state capital to Fort Des Moines. By 1856, the legislators from the eastern portion of the state had determined that their best chance was to deliver a bill that would annul all previous legislation on the subject of moving the capital. Unfortunately, no such moment presented itself that year. There was one desperate attempt at a gathering to discuss the development of the state constitution in 1857, but that injunction was quickly brushed aside, and the residents of the eastern half of the state were forced to resign themselves to the fact that their capital would soon be moving.[26]

While the residents of Johnson County were busy trying to keep the capital, the citizens of Polk County were vying for the ideal location. The legislative act that was signed by Governor Grimes on January 15, 1855, and made it possible for the capital to be moved from Iowa City to Polk County had one stipulation, which was that the new capitol must be constructed within two miles of the junction of the Des Moines and Raccoon Rivers. This was obviously music to the ears of former Fort Des Moines residents. When it came to the battle of acquiring the new capitol, East Des Moines business leaders, among them Dr. Alexander Shaw and Isaac Brandt, were quite determined to see the new landmark land on their side of the river. Historian Ilda Hammer reported that initially, the prospects did not look bright for those living on the east side of the Des Moines River. Much of the land "was a thick woods, where wolves, deer, and other wild animals still had their homes. The thickets so dense that a party of women became lost in it, and wandered about until late at night." Aside from the wild landscape, it was acknowledged that the eastern bank of the river had a tendency to flood when the river ran high.[27] Not to be deterred by these ecological factors, in 1854 some of the most powerful east side landowners banded together in order to launch a campaign to acquire the new capitol. Together, they managed to recruit "some of the most influential political and financial managers of the State" and ignite in them an interest in east side real estate. A Des Moines historian described the key to the east side victory in securing the state capitol:

> *The West Side had for a time looked on the new East Side movement with indifference, but soon to its surprise found itself face to face with a young but vigorous and ambitious rival, seeking to capture a prize for which the original town had fought so long and now supposed to be safely in its possession.... They* [the east siders] *had this advantage: Theirs was virtually a new enterprise and they had everything to gain. They were therefore, more united than were the residents of the original town* [west side of Des Moines], *worked better together and were more liberal in the offer of inducement* [to secure the capitol].[28]

A capitol site selection committee visited Des Moines in 1855 and explored various options on both sides of the river. On the west side, the committee considered Grimmel's Hill, which was surrounded by Fourth

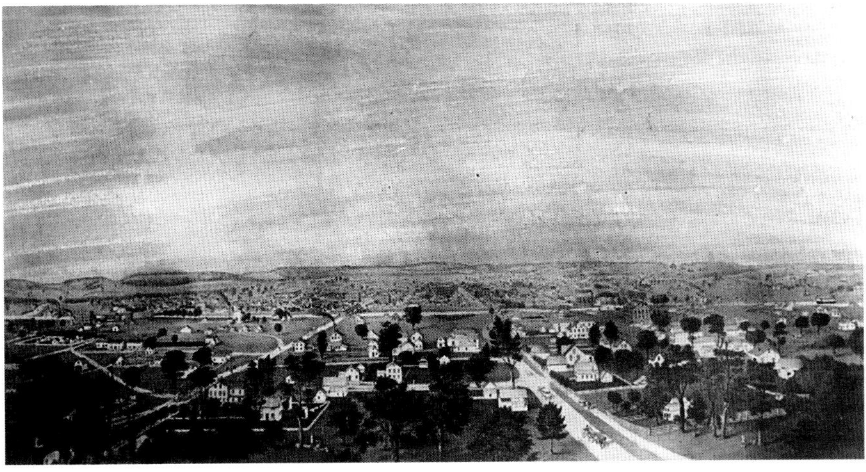

An early drawing of the eastern half of the city. *DMPL available through a CC-BY License.*

and Eighth Streets to the east and west and Grand Avenue and School Street to the north and south. This was a large and valuable plot of land, which explains why west siders were enraged to find out the committee had chosen to go with a smaller and less valuable location on the east side.[29] Surprisingly, there was a second east side contender for the new capitol. Dr. Thomas K. Brooks was one of the earliest settlers on the eastern banks of the Des Moines River and had founded the small town of Brooklyn, located near the present-day state fairgrounds. Dr. Brooks had earlier led a campaign to name Brooklyn as the seat of Polk County that was sadly unsuccessful. Not to be deterred, Dr. Brooks again campaigned oh behalf of Brooklyn as the new home of the state capitol. Unfortunately for the ambitious Dr. Brooks, his campaign was unsuccessful, and Brooklyn was eventually reabsorbed into the city of Des Moines.[30]

The east side ultimately won out not just because of the relationships the citizens had formed with prominent political leaders throughout the state but also because landowners on the east side were willing to pool together portions of the land and donate it to the state at no cost. William Alexander Scott donated the largest portion of the seventeen acres that made up the original capitol grounds in Des Moines. He also helped to pay the cost of building the new capitol. Scott's goodwill cost him considerably, and he died in 1859 on a trek to Pikes Peak, where he hoped to recoup his wealth.[31] While acquiring the capitol might have cost Scott greatly, the result was a beautiful new location for the state's centerpiece:

> *On one of the most commanding of these knolls the Capital* [sic] *Building is placed. Although its location has been the theme of much sharp contention between various rival interests, on the other side of the river, there is probably no spot where it could have been situated exceeding in natural advantages than the beautiful position it now occupies.*[32]

Selecting the east side as the home for the future state capitol was a sweet victory for east siders. Of course, the fact that the east side secured the site for the new capitol did nothing to increase goodwill with the western half of the city. Although it was one city, a feud had raged between East and West Des Moines since an 1846 election where the results for surveyor overturned an east side winner for a west side candidate.[33] Rumors circulated that east side business leaders had bribed the committee. These rumors led to some investigation, which in turn brought about resentment from east siders, who were insulted to have their character and hard-won victory dragged

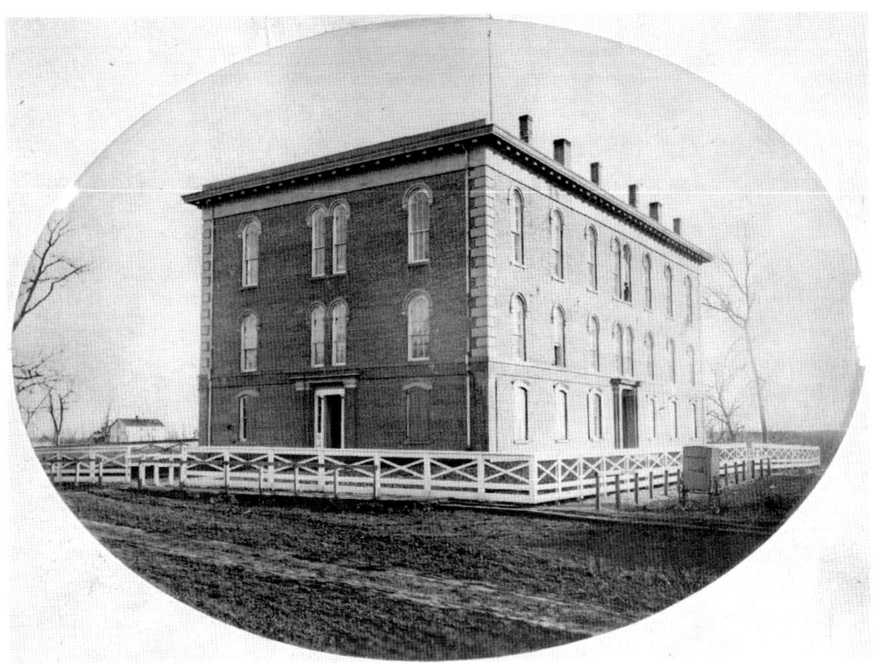

The first capitol building in Des Moines. *SHSI-DM: 6132.5.*

through the mud. Needless to say, the battle for the capitol did little to unite the city and, in many ways, actually stunted the bond between East and West Des Moines.[34]

After settling on a location in East Des Moines, the legislature then faced the logistics of physically moving all the belongings from the old stone capitol in Iowa City to East Des Moines. At this time, there was no railroad connecting Iowa City and Des Moines, so the only way to transport items was either by river or across land using a stagecoach. Since traveling by river was dependent on weather and fluctuating water levels, the legislature decided to go with the Western Stage Company. The Western Stage Company won out as it prided itself on overcoming all sorts of conditions and, frankly, because no one else really wanted the job of moving all the records and furniture from the old capitol to its new home 120 miles away in East Des Moines. In order to facilitate the move, men from Des Moines formed teams to help transport the four massive office safes to Des Moines. While the move was not easy and required traveling through snow, across impassable riverbeds and at times resorting to means of transport involving bobsleds and oxen, eventually the move to Des Moines was completed.[35]

The initial capitol in Des Moines was a simple three-story brick structure measuring fifty-six feet by one hundred feet. John C. Booth was appointed supervisor of the project; he then contracted work out to William Lowry, John Hyde and H.H. Rich, who were responsible for doing a majority of the construction in 1856. The original capitol in Des Moines included Ionic architecture, a stone foundation and windowsills and a tin roof. To celebrate the new capitol in Des Moines, there was a public celebration in which the American flag was hoisted to the top of the new building on July 4, 1857, even though the building was not yet complete. Construction on the capitol was finally completed in November 1857, and the general assembly was able to take up residence in the new building in January 1858.[36]

While the earliest settlers had avoided the eastern bank of the Des Moines River because of its tendency to flood, it appeared that the addition of the new state capitol proved incentive enough to draw new residents to East Des Moines. In his 1857 history of the city, H.B. Turrill noted:

> *Still, buildings are being erected throughout the whole bottom, on the slope of the hill where the Capitol is located, and even beyond it. The whole hillside and valley, from present appearances, will in a few years be entirely covered with houses. Some of those now erected are very fine and costly.*[37]

Acquiring the state capitol provided a tremendous boost in east side business. In 1858, a judge from Boone wrote to a friend, "The old town [west side of Des Moines] is ruined....The town of course goes there [to East Des Moines]." The judge also noted, "Now [West Side] business there is at a standstill and speculative [land] prices are tumbling down." Historian Will Porter also took note of the positive impact that the capitol construction had on East Des Moines between 1854 and 1857, saying:

> *The new town on the east side of the river had a remarkable growth during these three years and became to some extent, a rival of the West Side, or original town. This, together with the location of the capitol on the East Side...brought about much local feeling which for a time, engendered the animosities common to such rivalries.*[38]

Bringing the state capitol to East Des Moines meant some significant technological advances for the city as well. In 1864, gas streetlights came to Des Moines, and just a few years later in 1866, the first street railway system came to the city. This original line was a narrow-gauge horse-drawn line that

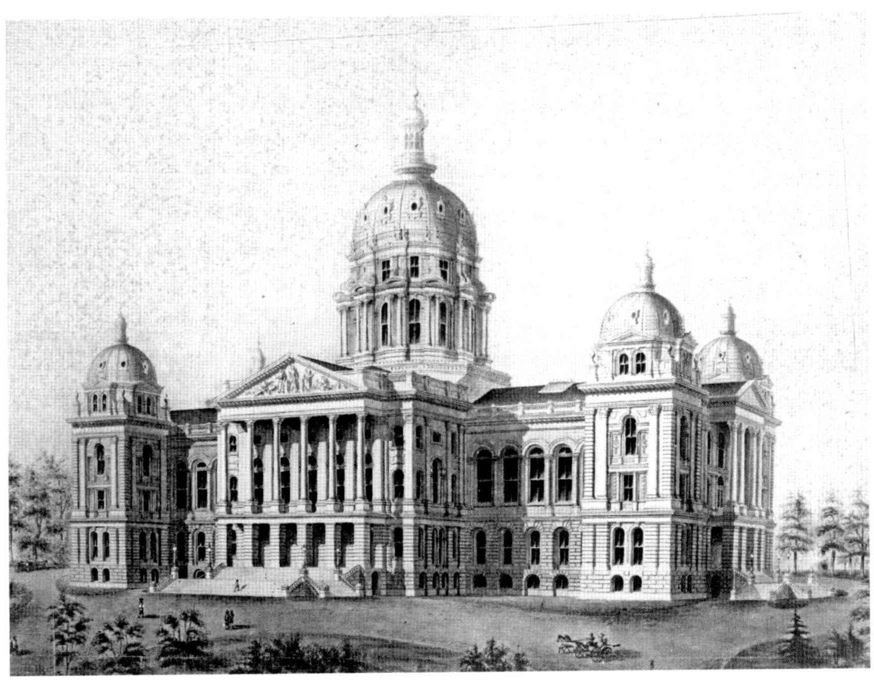

An architectural sketch of the proposed second capitol building in Des Moines. *SHSI-DM: 8897.2.*

ran from the capitol in East Des Moines to the courthouse on the west side of the river.[39]

By 1869, there was some interest in replacing the original Des Moines capitol building with a new and improved structure. The first capitol in Des Moines had been built rather quickly and the materials used were not of the highest quality, and as a result, the building had deteriorated rather quickly. Surprisingly enough, this sentiment was not shared by all the members of the general assembly, many of whom actually desired to move the state capitol to a third location such as Oskaloosa or Cedar Rapids. This decision on whether the capitol should be renovated or moved was put to a debate, and the deciding vote was cast by general assembly member Father John F. Brazil. Brazil was present, if somewhat intoxicated, and cast the necessary vote in favor of constructing a new capitol building.

Construction on the new capitol building began in 1873, but immediately the site was plagued with setbacks. The initial foundation had to be completely demolished, as it was realized too late that the stone used was of an inferior quality. When it replaced the foundation in 1873, the city also took this as

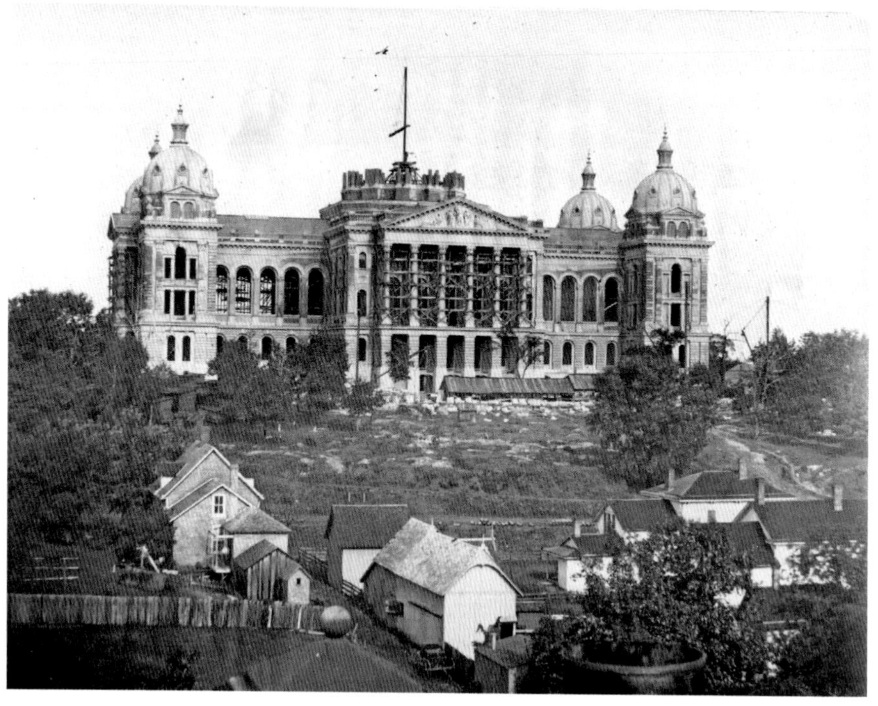

A photo of the second capitol building in Des Moines under construction. *SHSI-DM: 5000.121.*

an opportunity to host a ceremony for Governor Samuel Merrill to lay the cornerstone of the new capitol. The stone was a granite boulder from Buchanan County and measured 7 feet long, 3 feet wide and 3 feet thick. The architecture of the second capitol in Des Moines was very much within the style of the late nineteenth century. No expense was spared when purchasing materials to build the new capitol; stone such as granite, sandstone and limestone were sourced from all over the Midwest, including Illinois, Missouri, Minnesota and Ohio. Additionally, twenty-nine different types of marble were used to finish off the interior of the capitol; these marbles had been sourced from all over the world, from locations such as France, Germany, Italy and Spain. While many of the marbles in the capitol came from every corner of the globe, one of the most distinctive types of marble used in finishing off the capitol was the coral marble that came from Charles City, Iowa. Skilled craftsmen were brought in to create beautiful works of carved stone and wood to fill the interior of the capitol. The new law library was framed by two ornate five-story ironwork staircases. On top of all the decorative metal and woodwork, the new capitol was filled with various murals and intricate mosaics. Even some of the most

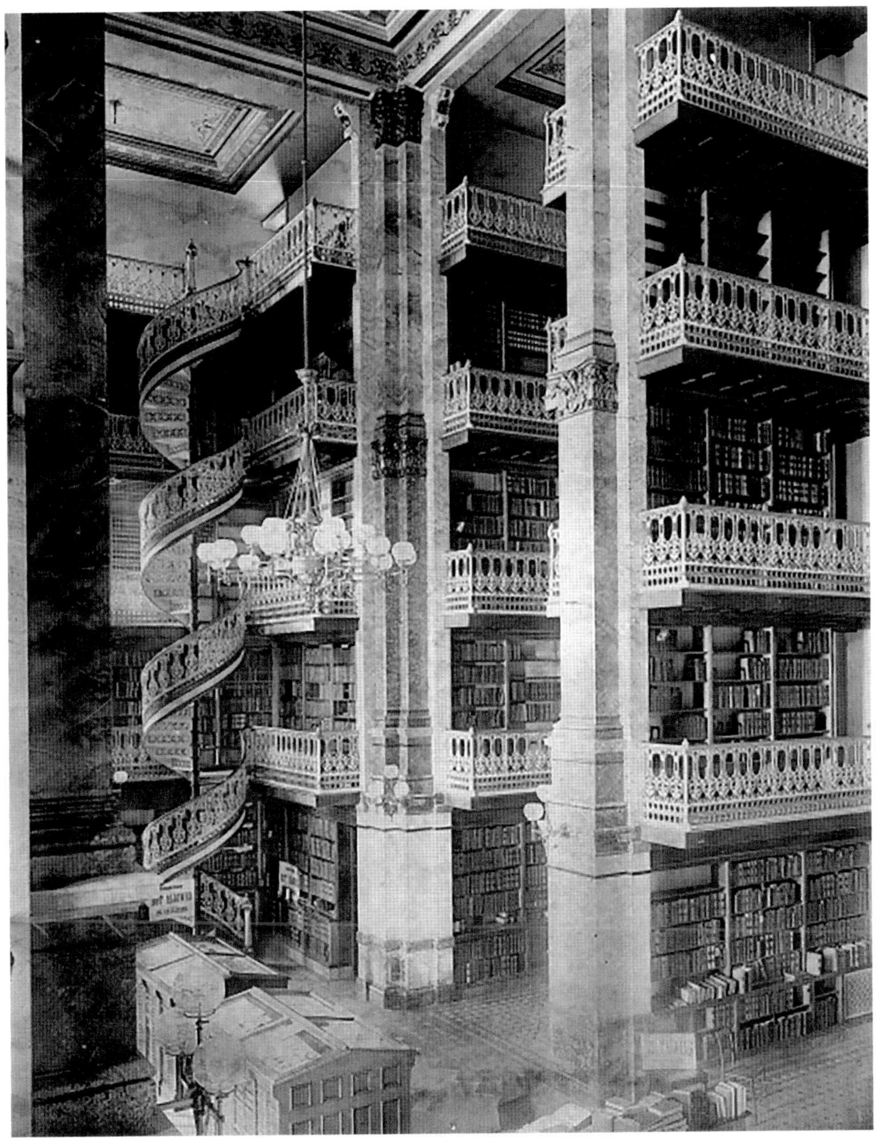

A view of the law library in the second capitol. *DMPL available through a CC-BY License.*

functional features of the capitol, such as the heating system, still maintained decorative elements. The building was heated using a steam system, but the architects still saw fit to include twenty-seven fireplaces throughout the new capitol. The piece de resistance of the new capitol was its shiny golden dome, which stood 275 feet from the base of the capitol.[40]

Finally, construction was completed, and the new capitol was dedicated on January 17, 1884. All in all, the new capitol cost a grand total of $2,873,294.59, with only $3.77 unaccounted for in the budget.[41] While there might have been some struggle to get the general assembly on board with a new capitol in Des Moines, the citizens of Des Moines were certainly pleased with the results. Local newspaper the *Journal* had the following to say about the construction of the new capitol building in 1875:

> *Our new State House looms in majestic proportions towards becoming the grandest building upon the most commanding site in the Western States. Strangers are drawn by its magnificent promise and by the general prosperity of the country which surrounds it, to seek homes and occupations in its shadow. Buildings of all sorts rise around it as if by magic and teem with business and family residences. Our streets swarm with activity from early morning till far into evening. They are obstructed upon every hand with building materials and moving*

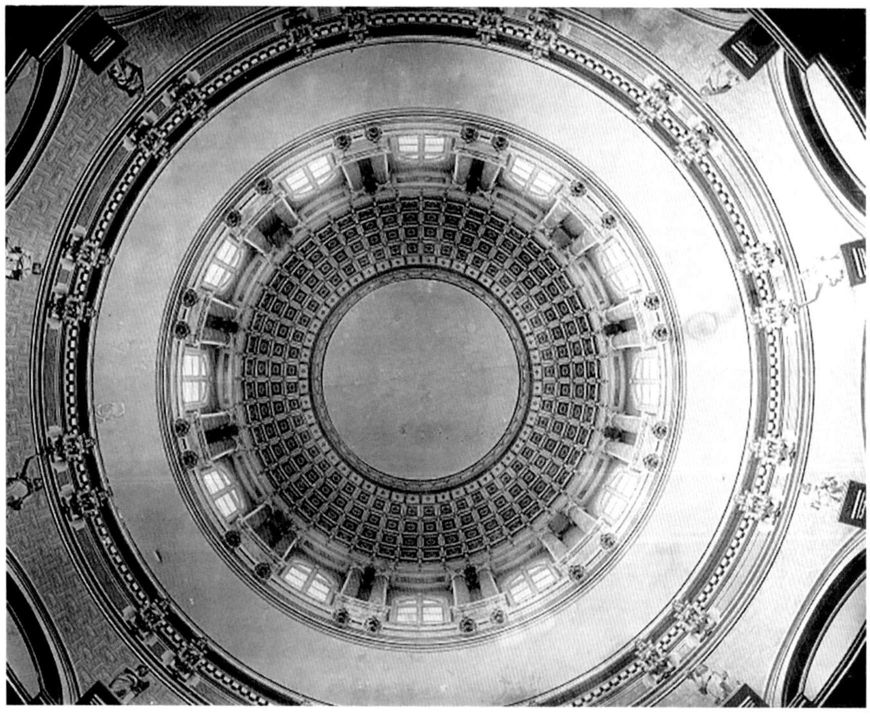

A photo of the interior of the dome of the second capitol. *DMPL available through a CC-BY License.*

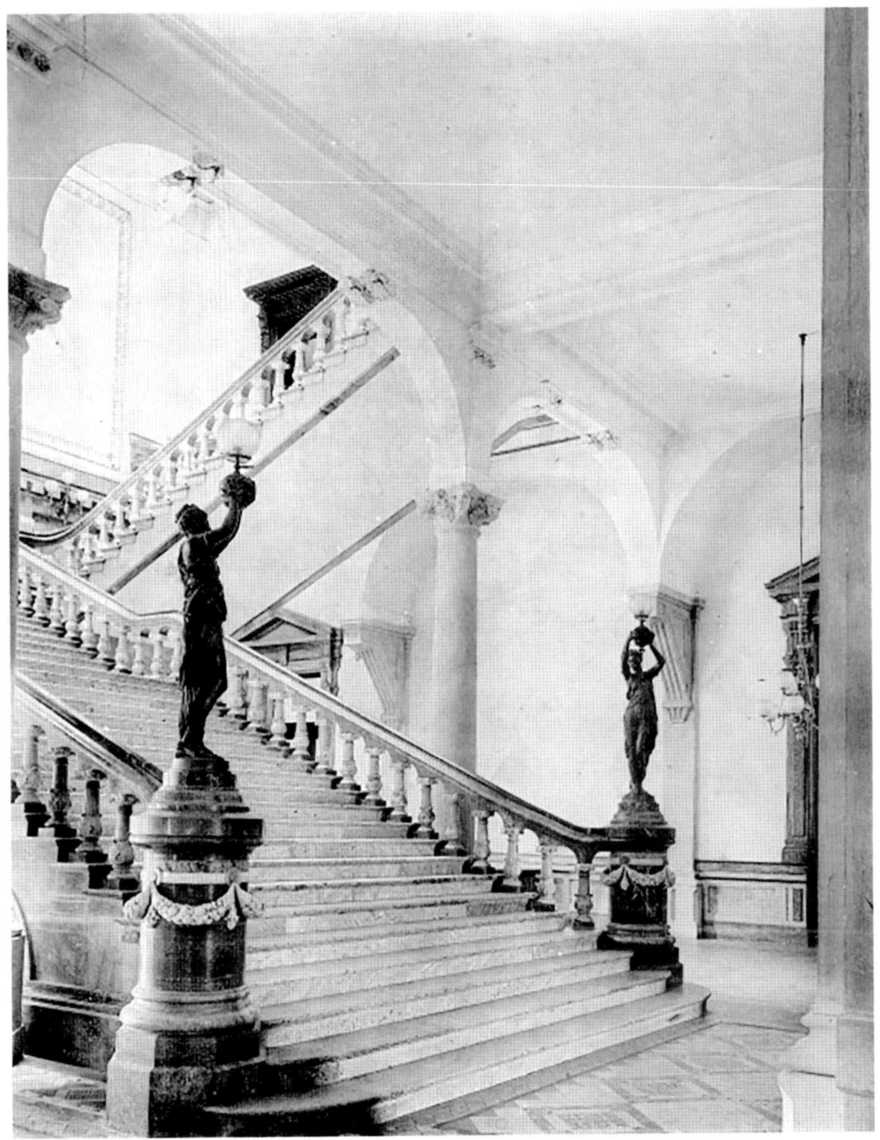

A photo of the grand stairway in the capitol. *DMPL available through a CC-BY License.*

horses. Farm wagons, coming with produce and going with implements and merchandise, throng the highways. Concentrating railroads empty out car loads of sellers and purchasers from surrounding villages. Our hotels and boarding houses over run with sojourners and commercial travelers. Des Moines is rapidly becoming the business and social center

> *of a great rich State which increases steadily and fast in population, in education, and in wealth.*[42]

As construction progressed on the second capitol building in Des Moines, the citizens of the city took note of the fact that Capitol Hill was starting to look a bit shabby. One point of contention was the historic Shaw house. Dr. Shaw's house had sat on the capitol grounds since 1854, when it initially served as a meeting place for state legislators during the general assemblies when Des Moines was still a young capital city. After the construction of the capitol building, the Shaw house served as a church and Catholic school for the children of East Des Moines before there was any formal church on the east side. Sadly, as time went on, the Shaw house fell into disuse and disrepair and attracted some less than desirable residents. In 1882, the *Iowa State Register* reported, "There was a sound of revelry by the Shaw mansion just south of the old Capitol yesterday afternoon where a drayman had gathered there a large quantity of furniture which he proposed to move in, despite the opposition of the numerous squatters who now occupy various

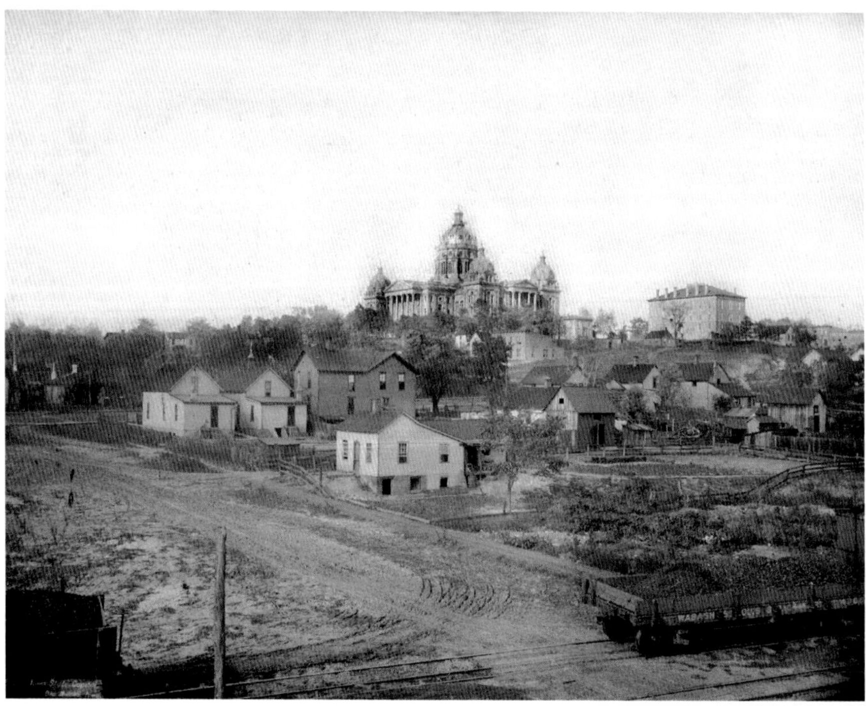

A rare photo of the new and old capitol buildings in Des Moines. *SHSI-DM: 18283.*

flats in the rickety rookery." Just a few years after this incident, it was decided that the Shaw house would be demolished in 1884, and developer George Garver replaced the house with a series of row houses.[43]

Since the construction of the golden-domed capitol, there had been much debate about what should be done with the original Des Moines capitol building. Initially, the state had attempted to sell or lease out the old capitol building, but with no luck. Over time, the original capitol deteriorated to the point where it was no longer inhabitable. Plans were made to tear down the old capitol, but fate ultimately decided, and on September 1, 1892, the building caught fire. It is unclear how the fire started, but after it was eventually put out, it was realized that the roof and entire third story had been completely destroyed by fire and water damage. Thankfully, parts of the old capitol were able to gain a new life; the brick from the old capitol was used to build the firewalls of the boiler room in the capitol heating plant. What lumber could be saved was used to build local sidewalks, and the rest was used for kindling. The remainder of the building had sustained considerable water damage in an effort to put out the fire and was beyond saving. While some

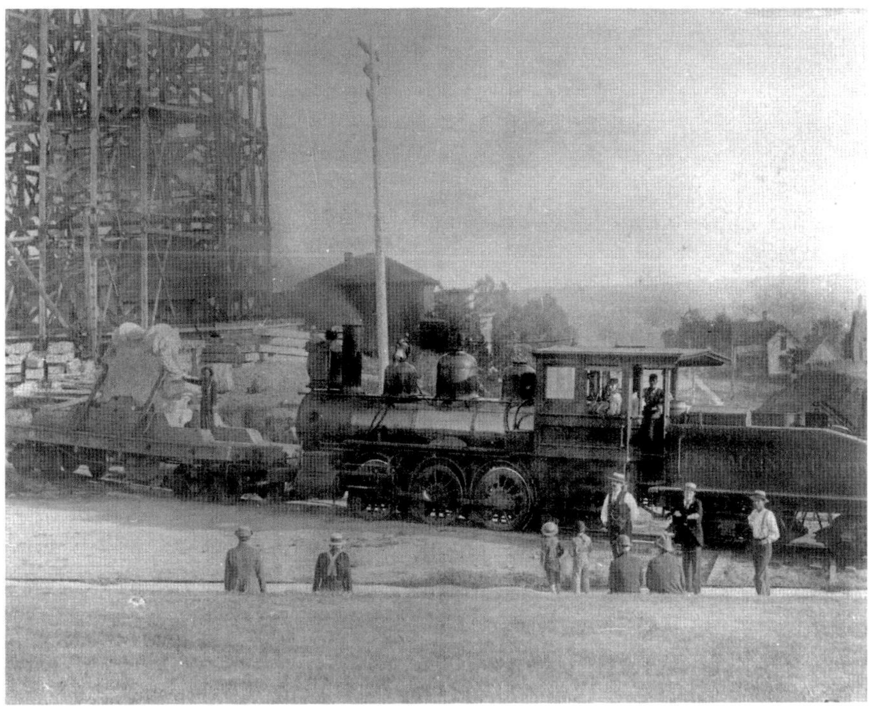

An image from the construction of the Soldiers and Sailors Monument. *SHSI-DM: 18075.*

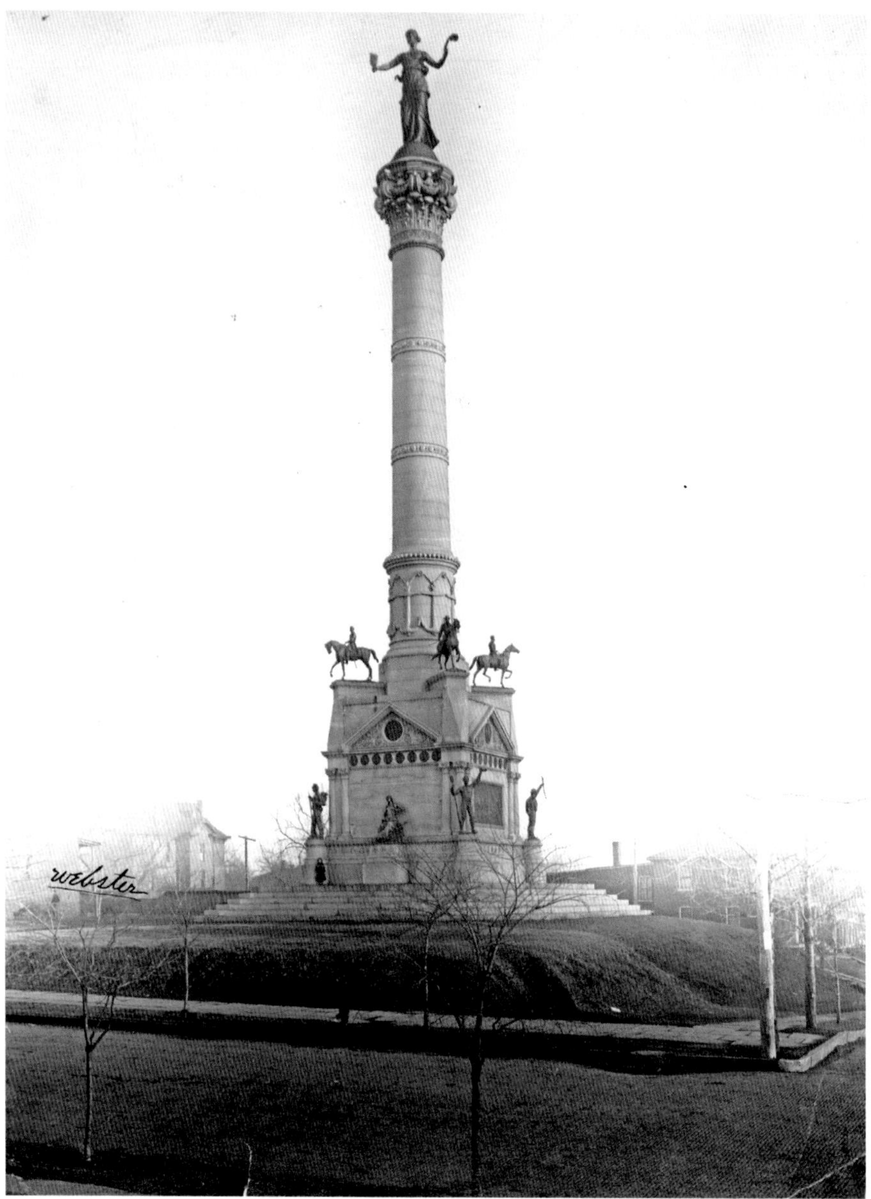

The completed Soldiers and Sailors Monument. *SHSI-DM: 5000.266.*

may have been sad to see the end of the first capitol, which had been home to thirteen general assemblies and two special sessions, others felt differently. Among them was the East Des Moines newspaper *Plain Talk*, which reported that "the building has been an eyesore for some time."[44]

After the old capitol building was destroyed by fire, it was proposed that the site host the new Soldiers and Sailors Monument. But, as with any decision, there was much debate centered on the placement of the proposed monument. The veterans of the city hoped to see the monument placed on the banks of the Des Moines River. Ultimately, it was decided that the monument would be a pleasant addition to the capitol grounds and was slated for construction just south of the capitol building. *Plain Talk* argued its support for this location, stating that "there was no more beautiful location for it." In order to facilitate the construction process, a railroad spur needed to be laid along East Ninth Street. Ultimately, as the monument neared completion in 1895, the citizens of Des Moines were encouraged by the unobstructed view of the new monument on the capitol grounds.[45] Even years after completion of the monument, there was still talk about moving the monument to the riverfront prior to the First World War; perhaps the indecision as to the location of the monument contributed to the fact that it was not officially dedicated until June 1945.[46]

In 1903, a third capitol commission was tasked with looking for ways to modernize the golden-domed capitol and bring it into the twentieth

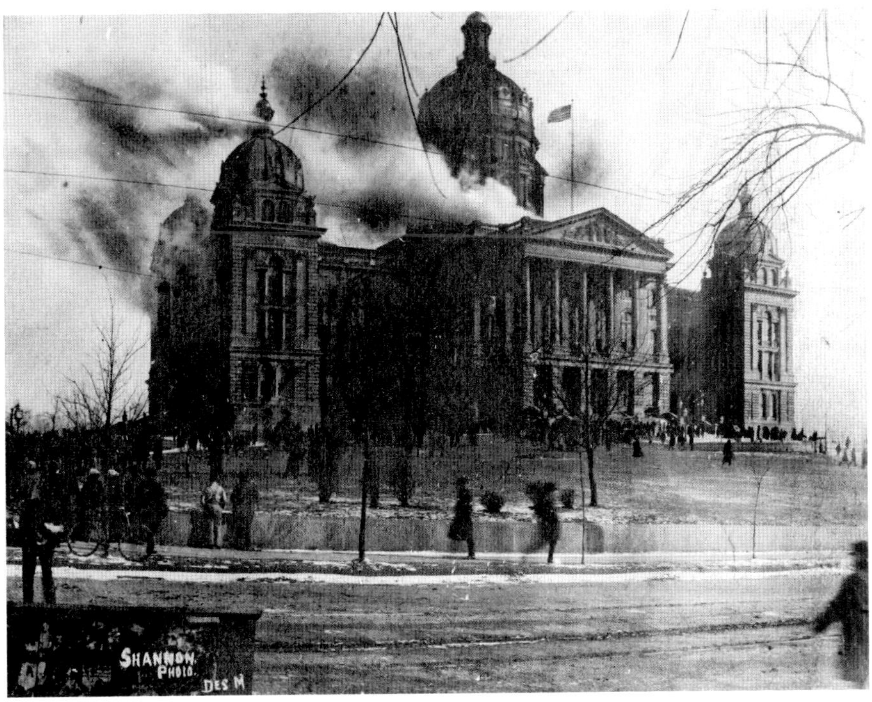

An image of the Iowa State Capitol during the fire of 1904. *SHSI-DM: 5000.255.*

century. As work began on the proposed renovations in 1904, disaster struck. A workman apparently left a candle unattended, which started a blaze in the House of Representatives Chamber. Firefighters tried to do their best to ward off the fire, but they lacked sufficient water pressure. The citizens of East Des Moines were anxious to save their capitol and assisted in removing approximately twenty to thirty thousand books from the law library. Ultimately, the fire resulted in approximately $400,000 to $500,000 in damages, primarily to the House of Representatives Chamber, with the ceiling being completely destroyed. Aside from the financial costs, the fire also created some logistical headaches for the general assembly. The Iowa legislature was due to meet just one week after the fire occurred, so a solution for where to house the representatives of the state needed to be found fast. Not to be deterred by the fire, the representatives of the House decided they would still meet in their chamber, regardless of the fire. In order to hide the damage, tarps were draped across the ceiling to hide much of the damage and the soot. In spite of the tarps, it was reported that many House members felt the need to take daily baths after spending their days in the smoky and sooty House chamber.[47]

Throughout the later part of the nineteenth century, the state continued to devote funds for the development of the capitol grounds. In 1890, the general assembly voted to allocate $100,000 for improvements to Capitol Hill. At the top of the list of improvements was regrading the capitol grounds. Contractor W.H. King took on this project. This task was very laborious, requiring massive drag teams of horses, and was a nuisance to the neighbors, many of whom complained about the dust raised by the project. Throughout the whole summer, all the offices inside the capitol were coated in dust, and homeowners in the surrounding area found it preferable to close up their homes and vacate for the summer. The project was thankfully completed by late October 1890, and by that winter, the east side residents were grateful for the work, as it had turned Capitol Hill into one of the best sledding hills in the city.[48]

By the start of the twentieth century, Grand Avenue was quickly becoming the political heart of downtown Des Moines. Just prior to

Opposite, top: A view of the House of Representatives Chamber. *DMPL available through a CC-BY License.*

Opposite, bottom: Much of the ceiling of the House of Representatives was destroyed in the fire of 1904. *DMPL available through CC-BY License.*

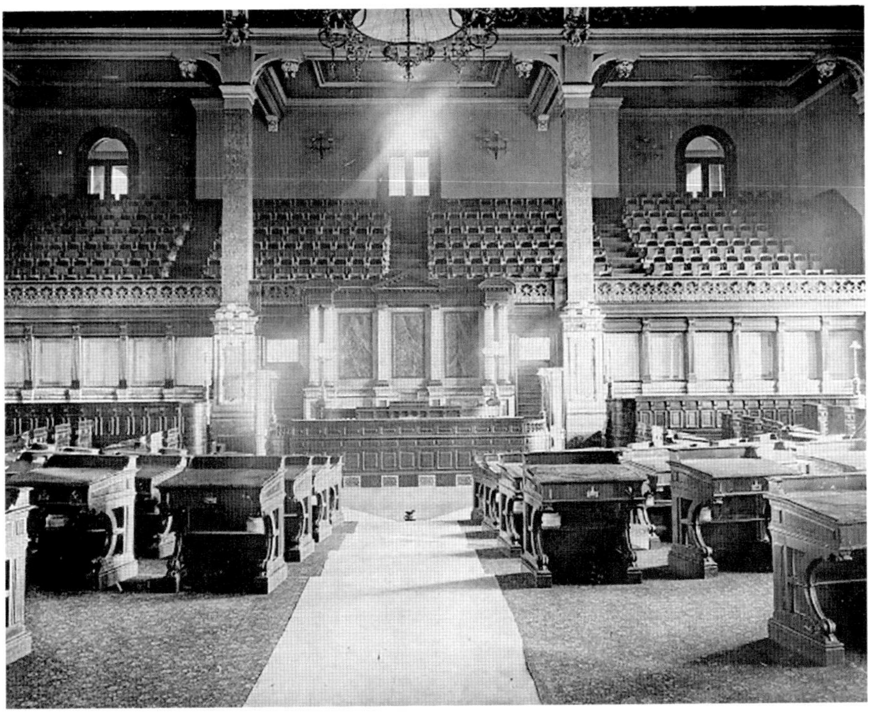

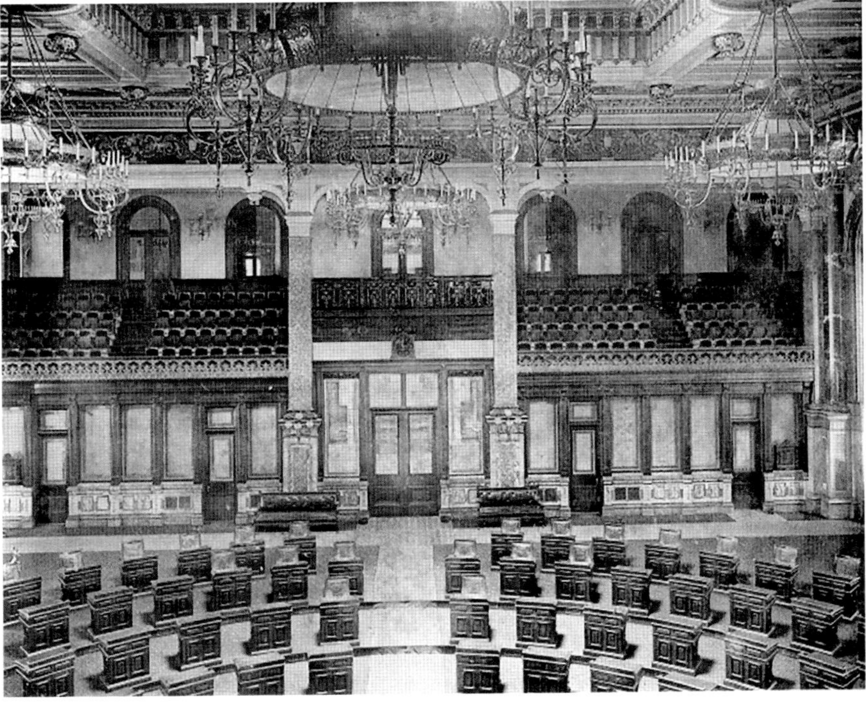

the turn of the century in 1899, the capitol expanded its grounds by purchasing a nearby plot of land at Eleventh Street and East Grand Avenue for the new State Historical Building. With this new addition, *Plain Talk* declared Grand Avenue to be "at the head of the leading streets" in 1905.[49] By 1910, Governor Beryl F. Carroll had called for the creation of a more comprehensive plan to organize the state government on Capitol Hill. Governor Carroll tasked architect Emmanuel L. Masqueray and sculptor Charles Grafly with the redesign of Capitol Hill. By 1913, the plans were complete, and the first phase of the redesign called for expanding the grounds of the capitol, removing some of the surrounding residential houses and laying the groundwork for a series of semicircular roadways around the capitol building; this latter plan was quite the change, considering that prior to the twentieth century the capitol was surrounded by various storefronts, tenement apartments and houses.[50] In that same year, the capitol grounds were also expanded from their original seventeen acres to sixty acres, which now extended east to Thirteenth Street, south to a line of bluffs and north to include the new site of the State Historical Building.[51] Local realtor L.A. Jester thought this expansion of the capitol grounds benefited the entire community, telling the *Register*:

> *There seems to be a general feeling that the purchase of property for the capitol extension and the clearing up of the unsightly conditions immediately surrounding the East side business district are having a decided effect in strengthening values and increasing the demand for property in the territory between the capitol extension and the center of the East side business district.*[52]

This interest in improving and developing the property surrounding the capitol continued throughout the twentieth century. Construction of a new state office building was completed in 1950 at a cost just shy of $5 million. The building was named the Robert Lucas State Office Building in honor of Iowa's first territorial governor, who served from 1838 to 1841. In order to increase usability of the building, a tunnel was constructed in 1953 for a little under $100,000 that connected the office building to the capitol.[53] The Iowa Workforce Development Building was finished in 1963. Just a few years later, in March 1966, the city began work on what would be the new Grimes State Office Building, named after Iowa's third elected governor. Governor Grimes held a particularly special place in the hearts of Des Moines citizens, as he was the governor who had approved changing the name from Fort Des Moines to Des Moines and designated the city as the new capital. The new building was located at the corner of East Grand Avenue and East Fourteenth Street, and construction was completed in 1968.[54] Expansion of the capitol complex continued into the 1970s, with the Jesse M. Parker Building constructed just northeast of the capitol in 1970 and the Hoover State Office Building finished in 1978.[55]

Many of these new additions helped to shape our modern understanding of the current capitol complex in Des Moines. Additionally, these new expansions helped to reshape the culture of the neighborhood surrounding the state capitol. Rather than being surrounded by local businesses and private residences, as the capitol complex moved closer to the twenty-first century, it was now nestled in the center of various structures that fed and supported state government, all of which lent an air of political importance to East Des Moines.

Chapter 3

State Fair

While securing a home for the new state capitol in East Des Moines was certainly a major accomplishment, east siders achieved another victory in 1885 when it was decided that the Iowa State Fair would establish a permanent home in the eastern half of the new capital city, approximately two miles from the capitol. Citizens of Des Moines were excited about this news and hoped that hosting the fair annually would mean an increase in profits and business for their half of the city.[56] Not only did the state fair bring more business to the city as a whole, but in particular it helped to spur the growth of businesses and homes in East Des Moines between the state capitol and the fairgrounds.[57] The fairgrounds are technically outside what is today considered to be the East Village, but the addition of the fairgrounds helped to shape the culture of East Des Moines and over the years became an integral part of the neighborhood.

Early Fairs

Prior to the introduction of the state fair, several counties throughout the eastern portion of the state hosted local county fairs. These fairs grew out of local agricultural societies that met regularly to share agricultural information among their constituents. The early fairs organized by these agricultural societies laid the groundwork for the state fair that was to come.

They centered on competitions showcasing the best in poultry, livestock and various types of grain, along with domestic and industrial arts. Through competition, these agricultural societies continued to raise the bar for agricultural and domestic outputs across the state.[58]

Deciding to permanently place the fair in Des Moines was quite the change. Prior to settling in Des Moines, the fair moved to different locations from year to year. The first state fair was held in Fairfield and only ran for two days, October 25–27, 1854. The original fairgrounds were made up of six acres marked off with a high fence, likely to deter anyone who might try to sneak in without paying. Admission to the first fair cost twenty-five cents, and the attractions drew an estimated seven to ten thousand visitors. Even with the tremendous number of visitors to the first state fair, the state agricultural society managed to lose money, due mostly to the fact that many attendees managed to swindle their way into the fair using counterfeit coins. Far and away the most successful event of the first fair was the female equestrian contests, in which women competed in horseback rides around a 1,500-foot oval track. The event was initially only planned for one day, but it was so popular among fairgoers that the organizers quickly scrambled to put together a second day of competition.[59]

The second state fair was again held in Fairfield, but after that it was decided the fair should change locations every two years. Muscatine hosted the state fair from 1856 to 1857; then Oskaloosa was home to the fair in 1858 and 1859. Next, Iowa City hosted the state fair in 1860 and 1861. Then there was a brief recess from 1862 to 1870, but the fair made a comeback in 1874 in Cedar Rapids. The state fair then moved north in 1874 to Dubuque but made its way back to Cedar Rapids again from 1876 to 1878. In 1879, the state fair finally made its way to Des Moines. The fairgrounds were set up in Brown's Park, which was a seventy-acre park between Thirty-eighth and Forty-second Streets, bordered by Center Street and Grand Avenue on the west side of the city. The fair in Des Moines lasted for eight days and drew a crowd of more than 100,000 people.[60]

Finding a Permanent Home for the State Fair

By 1884, there was interest in acquiring a permanent home for the state fair, with a strong preference for having the fairgrounds make their home in Des Moines. As with the move of the state capital, there was some resistance to permanently moving the state fair, primarily from the eastern residents of the state, who had grown used to easy access to the fair every year. Unfortunately for the eastern residents of Iowa, the legislature set aside $50,000 in order to purchase permanent fairgrounds, on the condition that the City of Des Moines was willing to contribute another $50,000 for any necessary improvements to the new fairgrounds. In hopes of keeping the state fair in Des Moines, prominent east sider Isaac Brandt stepped up to the plate and led a citywide campaign seeking pledges. He collected $51,000 from business leaders across the city. Interestingly, many of these pledges actually came from railroad companies. With the popularity of the state fair, railroads had been profiting substantially from the ticket fares of the thousands of fairgoers every year. By having a stationary location for the state fair, railroad companies likely assumed they would have a more stable stream of revenue and could potentially reinvest some of those funds into building up the railroads leading to the state capital.[61]

In 1885, it looked as though the city had found a new home for the state fair. East Des Moines farmer and cabinetmaker Calvin Thorton offered up his property as a potential site for the state fairgrounds. He had made his way to Fort Des Moines in the 1840s, and his 266-acre farm was the ideal location for the new fairgrounds. It was the highest point east of the new capitol, and Thorton had nicknamed the hill on which his farm sat "Inspiration Point." In June 1866, the state fair took possession of Thorton's property and quickly got to work making the necessary improvements. Almost immediately, the new home of the state fair fulfilled many of the economic hopes of East Des Moines citizens. Construction of the new buildings for the fairgrounds meant the creation of 150 new construction jobs. Along with new jobs, the construction on the new fairgrounds also brought a buzz of excitement to the eastern half of the city. On the night before the fair of 1886, a local newspaper noted, "A small town has grown up [in East Des Moines]....[The fairgrounds] has now all the appearance of a prosperous and booming village." As well it should! The construction crews had been hard at work all summer, and by September of that year, Thorton's former farm looked quite different; the developers of the fairgrounds kept four of Thorton's original buildings, but they also added thirty new buildings, along with fifty wells and a new half-mile-long racetrack.[62]

In constructing the new fairgrounds, the builders took advantage of Thorton's Inspiration Point. The sixty-foot hill offered a perfect view of downtown Des Moines, specifically the beautiful new capitol building. With this in mind, the State Agricultural Society selected Thorton's former

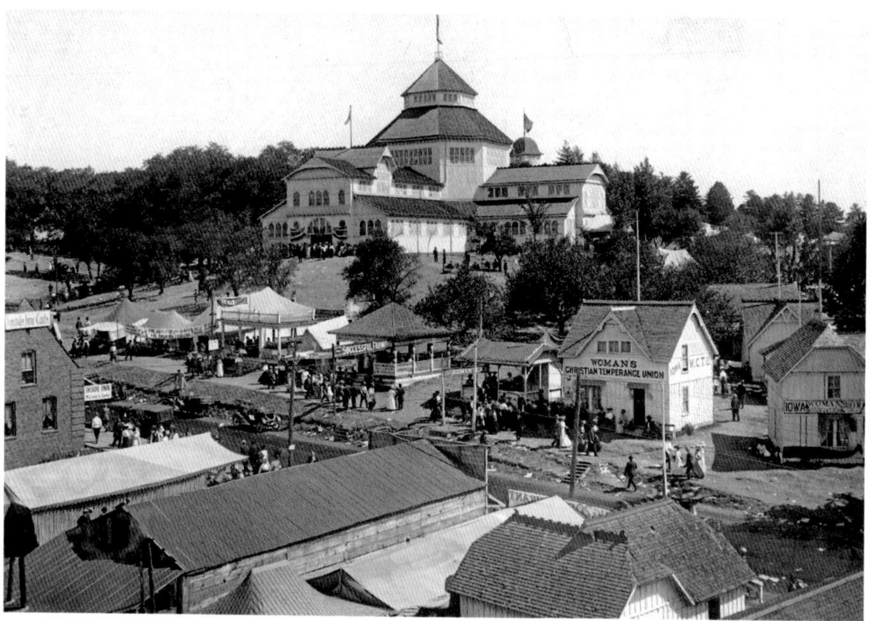

The new Exposition Hall on Thorton's "Inspiration Point." *SHSI-DM: 31179.*

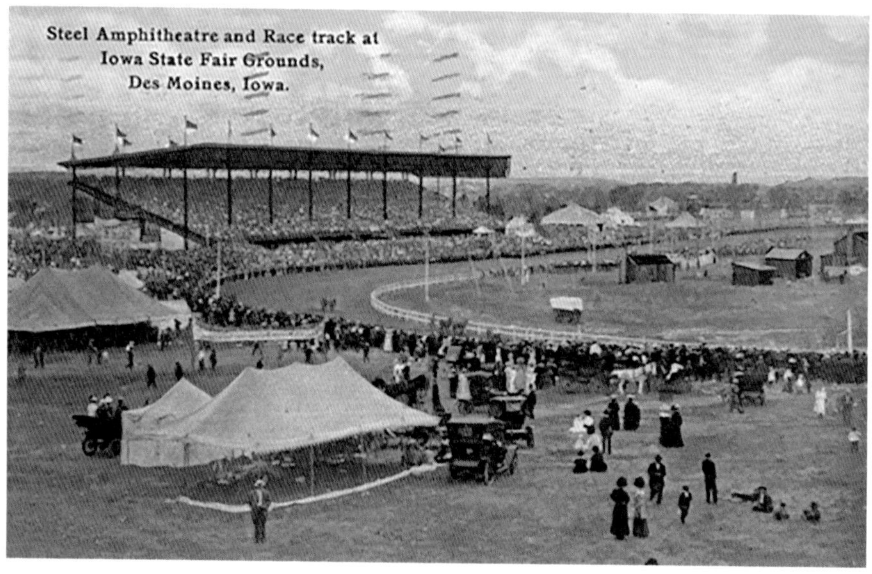

A historic postcard of the racetrack and amphitheater. *DMPL available through a CC-BY License.*

hill as the site for the highlight of the new fairgrounds: the ten-thousand-square-foot Exposition Hall. The agricultural society had grand plans for this building, which would be the heart of the agricultural exhibitions and events at the fair. Architect William F. Hackney was hired to design the building, and he shaped his plans around the designs for the Crystal Palace in London. On either side of the main hall, Hackney constructed two smaller pavilions, with the intention of hosting smaller fruit and floral displays here. The overall feeling of Hackney's final product was slightly religious in nature, with the new Exposition Hall resembling a church perched at the peak of the new fairgrounds.[63]

As the fairgrounds were in the process of being built, the city also began to consider altering the landscape of East Des Moines in order to better support the new state fair. Thorton's farm was located between what is now East Thirtieth and Thirty-sixth Streets and University and Dean Avenues. One major change that the city made was the expansion of Grand Avenue. Thorton was actually the one to suggest that this road lead directly from the future fairgrounds and into the heart of the city. Some also credit Thorton with suggesting the current name of Grand Avenue, which had previously been known as Sycamore. This thoroughfare would run parallel to the newly constructed grandstand on the fairgrounds, and expanding the street was

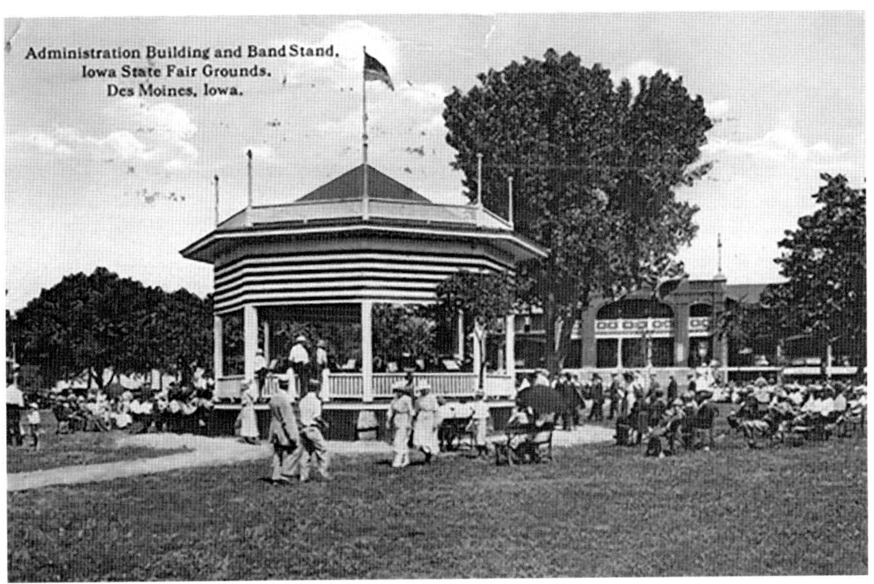

A historic postcard of the Administration Building and bandstand. *DMPL available through a CC-BY License.*

necessary in order to accommodate the influx of traffic the state fair would bring to the city annually. The expansion of Grand Avenue resulted in a street that was now seven miles in length and reported to be the "longest boulevard in the state" at the time.[64]

Upon entering the new Des Moines fairgrounds, visitors were immediately greeted by a half-mile-long racetrack. The new track measured seventy feet wide and was soon reputed to be "one of the finest and fastest tracks in the West." In order to house all the spectators, a large wooden amphitheater was constructed alongside the track. Adjacent to the track was a series of twenty-nine newly constructed wooden barns meant to house cattle, hogs and sheep at the fair. Funnily enough, one of the wooden buildings, which very closely resembled the barns used to house livestock, was actually a dormitory building for exhibitors at the fair. Interspersed between all the barns and the amphitheater were smaller lots for dining halls and other amusements at the fair. Over the next few decades, all but one of these initial wooden barns and buildings on the new Des Moines fairgrounds would be replaced with varying arrangements of barns. The amphitheater would undergo three renovations over the years to better house the wide varieties of entertainment that made their way through the state fair. Surprisingly, with all the renovations the fair has undergone since 1886, the general layout of the fairgrounds today is quite similar to the original layout plotted in 1886.[65]

Entertainment and Exhibitions at the State Fair

Entertainment has always been a primary attraction for fairgoers, but from the start, the officers of the agricultural society struggled to balance their mission for sharing the state's agricultural advances with fairgoers' desire for entertainment. From the earliest state fair in 1854, female equestrian events were far and away the most popular among fairgoers, described as "the most thrillingly interesting and sublimely beautiful spectacle, which has ever been presented within our border, if indeed it has ever been equaled in the history of our country." As the ride began, spectators from all over the state crowded against the rope barriers around the track to watch the riders. Ten female riders participated in the first race and were "splendidly arrayed in long and sweeping riding habits, with feathers and ribbons to match." They also all wore masks in order to disguise their identities. As they rode out onto the track accompanied by a mounted cavalier, the riders received a

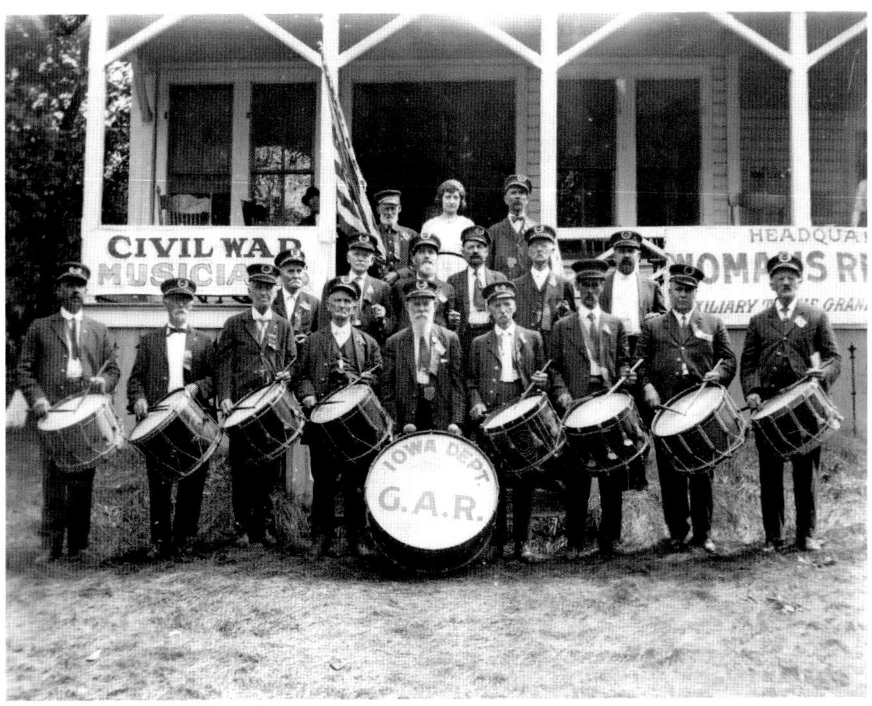

While there was much debate over appropriate entertainment, the 1900 Grand Army of the Republic Band was universally accepted by fairgoers. *SHSI-DM: 5000-513.*

brief lecture from the judges calling for ladylike and proper horsemanship. The contest then began, but it was not a traditional break-neck race around the track; instead, each of the ladies took turns riding around the track while the crowd cheered them on.[66]

There was some debate about the winner of the first female equestrian event. The performance of thirteen-year-old Eliza Jane Hodges from Iowa City was described as

> *the most dashing, terrific, and perfectly dare-devil performance ever witnessed on horse-back. The scene was thrilling, fearful—magnificent!* [Hodges] *mounted on her proud and untamable charger...flew around the course with the rapidity of lightning and with the sweeping force of a whirl-wind. And all this with a childlike smile upon her countenance and her whip in full play!*[67]

But the judges deliberated after the ride and agreed that the grand prize, a gold watch, should be awarded to "the most bold and graceful" rider,

Belle Turner from Lee County. At this news, the crowd erupted in shouts and jeers, showing their support of the young Hodges. Saddened that the young rider would lose out on the glory of winning the ride and the grand prize, the crowd quickly assembled $200 in donations to provide the young girl with a scholarship to a girls' school in Mount Pleasant. While the judges' decision was controversial, it aligned with the mission for the fair set forth by the state agricultural society. The judges argued that it was the job of the fair "to set an example by rewarding proper horsemanship, not daredeviltry."[68]

Even with the controversy over the judges' decision, the female equestrian event was a massive success. While many worried that the event promoted values that were not consistent with the agricultural mission of the fair, the agricultural society argued that it would continue to host the female equestrian event in an effort "to foster improvement in Iowans' horsemanship." That being said, the officers of the agricultural society shared some fairgoers' concerns about the propriety of the event and made it clear that the next year's event, in 1855, would not act as an event "to encourage ladies to train themselves for the Circus, or to perform daring feats of horsemanship." The judges claimed that they would only accept "graceful, easy riding, such as may be practiced in our cities, in our towns, on our high ways, without danger or Fear, and with perfect regard to graceful and healthy exercise."[69]

While the judges and agricultural society members assured Iowans that the female equestrian event would work to promote superior horsemanship throughout the state, there were still some holdouts. A primary dissenter was the agricultural society's secretary, John Wallace. Wallace did not approve of the female equestrian event, but his concerns were not focused on the propriety of the event. Instead, he was concerned that the popularity of the event was drawing fairgoers away from all the scientific agriculture exhibits that the agricultural society was trying to promote. At Wallace's insistence, the female equestrian event was dropped from the state fair's program in 1857. It would reappear every so often over the next few years; sometimes, fairgoers would even hold their own unofficial female equestrian events on the fairgrounds, right under the noses of the agricultural society officers! The female equestrian competition did make a reappearance at the 1880 state fair in Des Moines, but the event had quite the scandalous outcome. The $300 pot for the competition that year was enough to entice professional rider Nellie Burke to compete at the Iowa State Fair. Unfortunately, her entrance in the competition scared off any other women from entering the ride. In hopes of saving the event, a local woman named Miss Boyd kindly signed up at the last minute to compete against Nellie Burke. Since Boyd's entrance in the competition was so sudden, she was not sufficiently prepared for the ride. Fair officials scrambled to find her a mount and put together an appropriate riding outfit. In the end, Boyd was unable to control her willful mount and keep her ill-fitting riding habit on, and she ended up "exposing her person in a most disgusting manner." Thankfully, a fire marshal came to Boyd's aid and led her horse off the track while she tried to maintain some shred of modesty.[70]

With female equestrian events falling out of favor, fairgoers were in search of a new and exciting exhibition. In 1911, Iowan Mary Watts had an idea for a new competition at the Iowa State Fair. While wandering around the Audubon County Fair, Watts noticed an interesting contrast: the livestock at the fair seemed very hearty and healthy, but the people visiting the fair seemed to be lacking in comparison. Watts suggested that the state fair should focus not just on the newest and best techniques for raising livestock and crops but also on the latest and greatest techniques in raising children; from there, the idea for the best baby contest was born. In 1911, fifty mothers from across the state agreed to have their babies compete for the best baby in Iowa. For several years beforehand, the fair had offered a baby beauty pageant, but this was to be nothing like it. Instead of focusing purely on the physical appearance of a baby, this new competition was to be based solely on the science behind raising a healthy child. In order to assess the contestants' health, Dr. Margaret Clark of Waterloo was tasked with developing a scorecard, which she modeled after the scorecard judges used to assess livestock.[71]

To preserve the scientific nature of the first best baby competition, judges examined the babies behind closed doors, and even the winner was kept out of the public's gaze. Regardless of all the secrecy surrounding the judging, the state fair of 1911 was buzzing with excitement about this new competition. Officers of the state agricultural society were so pleased by this response that for the 1912 state fair, they made the competition an official part of the fair's program and added the additional incentive of a $500 prize for the winner. In order to boost the publicity of this new exhibition at the state fair, the officers also realized that they would likely need to make the event more accessible to fairgoers. As a result, an auditorium was constructed so that visitors to the fair could witness the judging of the best baby contest. This new auditorium featured judging rooms lined with glass walls and also offered spaces where physicians and other experts on childrearing could come and deliver lectures on the benefits of a "scientific" approach to raising children.[72]

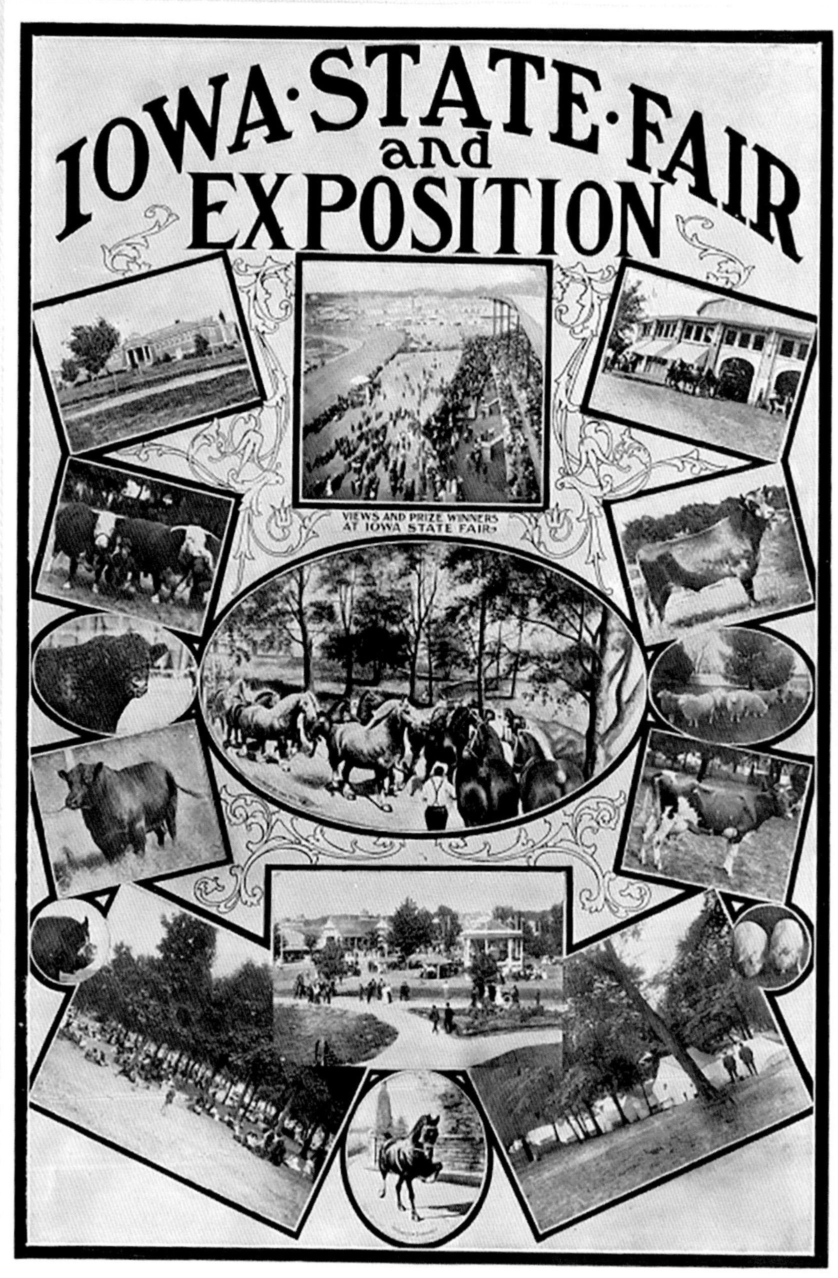

A poster featuring events and exhibitions from the state fair. *DMPL available through a CC-BY License.*

With the construction of this new auditorium, the best baby competition quickly skyrocketed in popularity and became an instant favorite of fairgoers. By 1916, the state fair was receiving approximately five hundred applicants for the contest annually. By the 1920s, the judges were so overwhelmed by the incredible number of applicants that fair officials determined it was necessary to put a cap on the number of babies that could be entered in the contest every year. Comparable to today's butter cow, visitors to the fair would line up to watch the judges examining the contestants. On the one hand, the popularity of the best baby contest could be explained by the newness of the contest and the fact that a baby is likely cuter than a hog or a cow. But the success of this new exhibition was also likely because it explored a previously untouched area of women's lives. The state fair offered many exhibitions that showcased women's handiwork around the house, but childrearing was a subject that had never before been discussed. In fact, prior to the institution of this exhibition in 1911, mothers were actually encouraged to keep their babies away from the state fair, as it was considered an unhealthy environment. Not only were fairgoers curious to see the adorable little babies and to understand what judges deemed to be "best," but women at the fair were also eager to sit in on the lectures led by childrearing experts from around the country.[73]

When it came to looking for the best baby in the state, the judges took into account a variety of factors. The *Register* joked that the judges obtained so much information from their examinations, but it was only "vitally important to the psychologists, nonunderstandable to the worried mamma and just a joke to the babies." One particular examination consisted of presenting the baby with a series of common toys, and the judges would evaluate the ways in which the baby interacted with the toys. As the contest progressed later into the twentieth century, judges expanded their evaluation categories to include the child's intelligence and personality. Interestingly enough, the judges were not looking for the smartest or most engaging child but, rather, the most mediocre baby. According to the judges, the best baby shouldn't be too bright, but not too stupid; they should not be disinterested in their toys, but excessive interest was concerning. One judge commented, "A brazen child is marked off as many points as one who is too shy. We would rather have a child move slowly and be more natural than be over sophisticated. Sophistication is a danger signal."

Not surprisingly, like any popular event at the fair, the best baby competition created some tension, specifically between rural and urban residents of the state. Since the state fair was an arena in which the rural members of the state showed off the products of their labors, the organizers of the fair expected rural babies to come out on top. With the popularity of the event, though, many urban mothers also entered their babies into the competition. What was shocking to the fair organizers was that for the first few years of the competition, the urban babies outscored the rural babies across the board. Of course, there were several explanations as to why this was the case. The judges complained that rural parents clung too tightly to old-fashioned wisdom about raising babies and were more likely to rely on "home remedies instead of availing themselves of modern medical science." In response, rural parents argued that the competition was prejudiced, since "city bred folks" often acted as the judges.[74]

The best baby competition and the female equestrian events had a few things in common; first, both events loosely tied into the agricultural mission of the fair set forth by the state agricultural society. Second, both had elements that created a bit of controversy. Finally, and probably most importantly, these events were widely popular, drawing massive crowds and bringing in substantial revenue for the state fair. Incorporating entertainment into the fair had been a point of contention for the officers of the state agricultural society since the fair's inception. While the officers called for a purely agricultural and educational event, the large crowds tended to draw various other sideshows and festivities. For earlier fairs, the officers allowed some sideshows the "privilege" to host shows outside the official fairgrounds, but the fair's organizers worried that allowing entertainment into the fair would draw in an unsavory crowd. An 1857 report outlined these concerns that "on occasion of State Fairs, great numbers of vagabonds always assemble to make their money by wits; by stealing, gambling, or some other almost equally objectionable method." Fair organizers' concerns were not unfounded; aside from attracting con men, the state fair also had a tendency to attract a wide variety of vice. Police often reported that they saw an increase in the number of men and prostitutes found in saloons and dens of ill repute throughout the city. In 1906, the police led a raid on East Court Avenue, and the *Des Moines Register and Leader* reported that "the houses were all stocked, it was claimed, to meet the big state fair patronage."[75]

Whether or not to allow amusements at the state fair was a hotly debated issue for many years; finally, financial motivations won out, and there was no arguing the fact that entertainments drew more fairgoers annually, which meant greater funds for the agricultural society. Though fair offices had determined that they would allow entertainments into the state fair, finding the correct formula was more difficult than expected. Throughout the later part of the nineteenth century, agricultural society officers waffled back and forth as to how to manage sideshows. Some years, officers would require sideshows to reserve lots; other years they would try to segregate the entertainments away from the agricultural exhibitions. In 1870, the officers

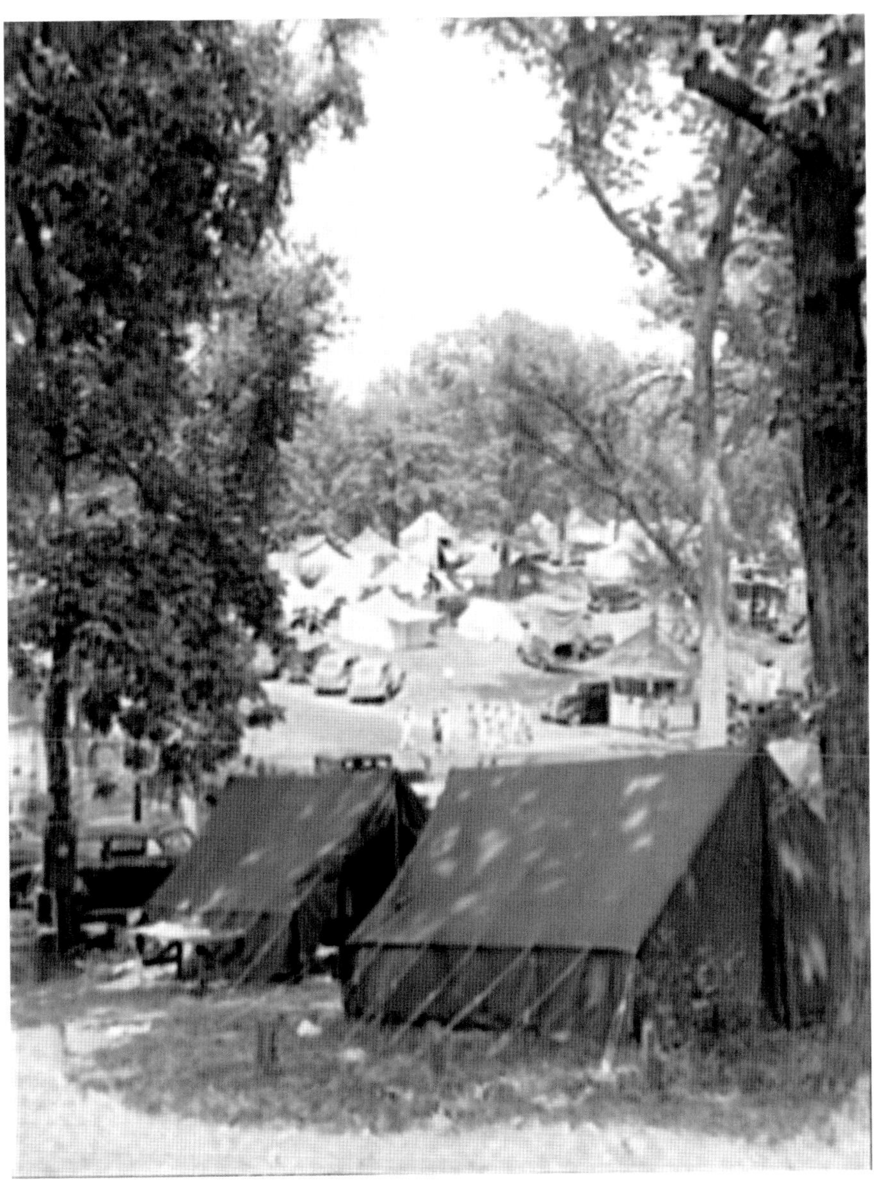

The campgrounds at the Iowa State Fairgrounds. *Library of Congress, Prints & Photographs Division, FSA/OWI Collection LC-USF34-027983.*

of the fair had voted to exclude all forms of entertainment for the year, but then at the last minute the officers panicked, believing that the fair would be a complete disaster without any kind of entertainment, and they had to scramble to line up performers three days before the fair. One particularly bad experience was the Pompeii exhibition of 1893. The fair's secretary, John Shaffer, planned to have a nightly fireworks display in downtown Des Moines to mimic the eruption of Mount Vesuvius. Everyone was incredibly excited by the idea, and the *Register* anticipated "that the nightly torrent of lava would increase attendance at the fair." Unfortunately for Shaffer, the fact that the fireworks display took place downtown meant that fairgoers left the fairgrounds and migrated downtown to view it, which resulted in a tremendous loss in revenue for the state agricultural society.[76]

Learning from their mistakes, the state agricultural society decided that any future entertainments hosted by the state must draw visitors to the fairgrounds and keep them there. Instead of moving fairgoers throughout downtown, the officers of the fair decided to invest their funds in massive productions on the grandstand stage. In 1902, the state fair hosted what was known as a "gargantuan disaster spectacle" and made the risky decision of going with a Mount Vesuvius theme once again. Unlike the show from 1893, this event kept visitors at the fair and included a major pyrotechnics display of the burning of ancient Rome on the grandstand. Thankfully, the fair's second attempt at Mount Vesuvius was much more successful, and disaster spectacles became a mainstay of state fair entertainment for the next thirty years. By 1910, the state fair had clearly turned a corner; fair organizers were now spending thousands of dollars every year to acquire the best and most exciting acts. Likewise, advertisements for the fair prominently featured all the upcoming shows and performers rather than any of the livestock or agricultural exhibitions. Fair officers also started outsourcing entertainment to sideshow companies rather than trying to recruit acts one by one. These companies could provide a broad range of entertainments; for example, the 1919 state fair featured an aquatic troupe of performers called Stella and Her Submarine Girls; an act called Don Carlo's Dog, Pony and Monkey Hotel; and the Big Wild West Show and Indian Congress for the grandstand.[77]

As the fair moved into the later part of the twentieth century, more specifically the 1980s and 1990s, some Iowans worried that it was too stuck in the past and wondered if something should be done to reinvigorate it. One suggestion was to find a new location for the state fair; this new location would obviously include a whole new set of buildings and attractions in hopes of breathing new life into the traditional state fair. Thankfully, that idea was quickly shot down by a huge outpouring of support from not just the residents of East Des Moines but also people across the state who "consider the fairground far more than a collection of buildings" but a cultural and historical gathering place that deserved to be preserved. Donors from all over the state offered up funds large and small to help reinvigorate the state fairgrounds in East Des Moines. Today, the Iowa State Fair continues to be a national favorite, earning the title of "America's Favorite Fair" in 2005. Through all the ups and downs, the Iowa State Fair has always held a special place in the hearts of those living in East Des Moines, and in honor of the neighborhood that has hosted the fair for so many years, the first Friday of the state fair for many years has been known as East Side Night, where the tightknit and family-oriented community gathers to celebrate its east-side pride.[78]

Chapter 4

Red Lights of East Des Moines

While there was certainly a lot of positive growth and development in East Des Moines, with the addition of the state capitol and the state fairgrounds, all of this growth brought with it some less than desirable side effects. When the capitol moved to Des Moines in the 1850s, there was increased public concern about some of the more improper changes taking place. An article titled "A Few Sober Thoughts for East Des Moines and Friends of Humanity in General" ran in the local newspaper. The author chose to keep his or her identity anonymous, going simply by "Citizen," but made it clear that the primary concern was the house of prostitution located at the base of the new Capitol Hill. The house was apparently run by "a man whose heart is black as Hell and who stalks abroad at noonday—dressed in finest clothes. He may be seen lurking about houses in this city for the purpose of enticing young and innocent girls from the path of virtue to the shades of death." The citizen's letter did not die there; it inspired public action, and the "fiend" who ran the house of prostitution at the base of the capitol was eventually arrested, tried and convicted.[79] Unfortunately for the citizens of Des Moines, the "fiend" near the capitol was not an isolated incident. In 1862, the *Iowa State Register* ran the following notice:

> *There was a tall, festive individual stalking around town yesterday morning, occasionally stroking his affluent whiskers, and inquiring in a significant manner for the whereabouts of institutions which are supposed to be highly disreputable. The young man's moral character seems to be suffering. For a*

> *stranger to approach respectable citizens and make such libidinous inquiries, argues an impudence and a moral depravity approaching the sublime. A proper response to this fellow would be to batter his gable end with an annihilating kick!*[80]

As the city of Des Moines grew in size and became a central hub for business and politics throughout the state, all that growth came with some less than desirable consequences. Prostitution, gambling, saloons and dens of ill repute were part of the growing pains that many developing cities across the country dealt with throughout the nineteenth century, and Des Moines was no different. No corner of the city was spared from the spread of prostitution, as the *Iowa State Register* described in 1886:

> *We are informed by an officer that there are six or seven other frail daughters of Eve…who distribute their favors first on one side and then on the other side of the river. Their residence seems to be that aggregation of thickets and timber which may be seen any day all around this city. They lead a sort of gipsy life and have the grass for their beds, and overhanging branches and the canopy of the skies.…They have control of a skiff, and almost every day they recreate between the west and east sides.*[81]

Geography of Vice in Des Moines

There were three primary centers of prostitution throughout downtown Des Moines. The largest and most notorious red-light district in the city was known as Whitechapel. Taking its name from the notorious London neighborhood where Jack the Ripper roamed, Whitechapel was located primarily on Elm Street and Pelton Avenue, just south of the downtown center near the junction of the Des Moines and Raccoon Rivers where Martin Luther King Jr. Parkway exists today. It is said that the neighborhood originated in 1884; as the city was developing around the railroad, real estate agent Ira P. Wettmore believed that there was a profit to be made in providing housing to railroad men and their families near the tracks. Wettmore's two-story brick and stone building rented quickly, but it was not long until vice made its way into the neighborhood. In 1886, a railroad man was called into court for operating a brothel out of his rented property; over the next five years, the neighborhood quickly degraded to the point where it was known as "the most notorious kind west of Chicago." The second red-light district of the city was located in the western half of downtown Des Moines. Many of the houses of ill fame congregated around West Third, Walnut and Cherry Streets, the latter of which, interestingly enough, was quite close to the county courthouse.[82]

In East Des Moines, much of the vice was centered on Court Avenue. Throughout the 1870s, many of the houses of ill fame were scattered throughout the eastern half of the city; while some of these dens of ill repute were positioned closer to the new state capitol, many tended to stay closer to the river, residing on the first and second blocks of many of the major thoroughfares. This was likely so that they would have easy access to both halves of the city. One madam, Mary O'Dell, was quite opportunistic and in 1875 was accused of operating two houses of ill fame; both houses were on East Walnut, but one was located between First and Second Street, while the other was located at the corner of Eighth Street, placing it just at the southwestern corner of the current grounds of the state capitol.[83]

Beginning in the 1880s, much of the prostitution in East Des Moines began to congregate around the first and second blocks of Court Avenue. Between 1879 and 1909, the State of Iowa brought charges against thirty-nine parties for crimes related to prostitution, all of which occurred on Court Avenue. These crimes included prostitution, keeping a house of ill fame, frequenting a house ill fame and being a public nuisance. Another interesting charge that the state regularly leveled against citizens was "leasing houses for the purposes of prostitution," which held landlords responsible for knowingly allowing their tenants to operate houses of ill fame.

SCANDAL IN THE SENATE

Having red-light districts within reach of the state capitol was due to cause a bit of scandal. One particularly memorable incident occurred in February 1892. On February 19, just after the senate adjourned around noon, a fight broke out between state senator Finn and a senate doorkeeper and political correspondent, H.M. Belvel. Just the day before, Belvel had written an editorial that appeared in local papers across the state, alleging that Finn had been found in a notorious local brothel the Saturday before. Belvel wrote, "Finn is a pink to be put forward to talk for temperance and virtue… notorious libertine and common blackguard that he is." As the morning

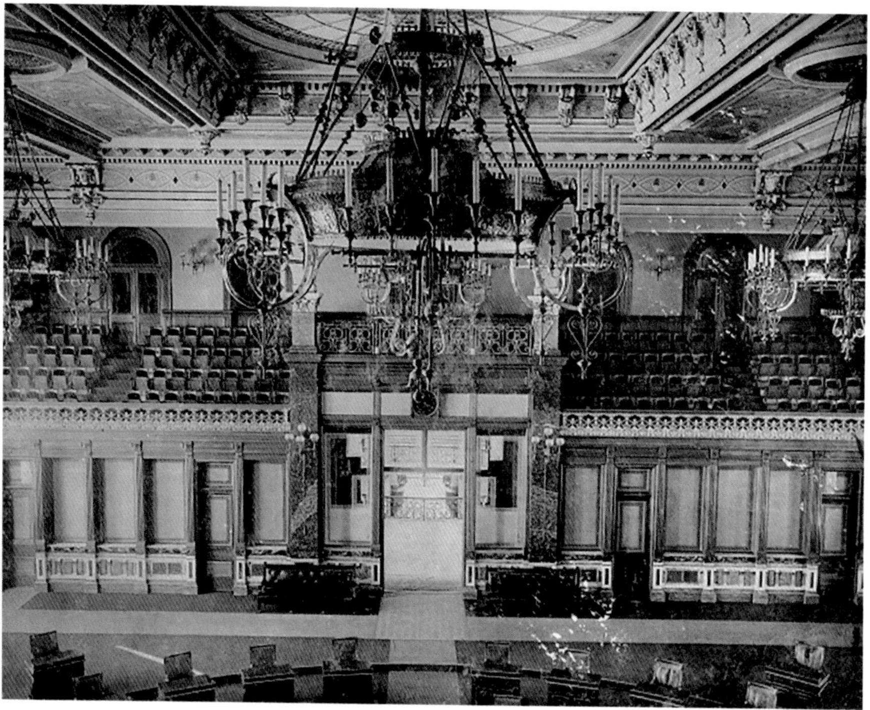

The senate chamber where Finn and Belvel's fight broke out. *DMPL available through a CC-BY License.*

session came to a close, Finn approached Belvel and pulled him to the side of the chamber to privately discuss the matter. Reports claim that initially Finn began by chastising Belvel for his lies, but when Belvel quickly interjected, claiming that he had been telling the truth, Finn became enraged. He called Belvel a "dirty dog" and proceeded to knock him to the ground and laid into him with his fists. Soon, what had begun as a quiet discussion between two men was a mass of senators and reporters trying to tear the two fighting men off each other.[84]

After the knock-down, drag-out fight on the senate floor, a reporter from the *Des Moines News* was able to interview both Belvel and Finn, and it appeared that neither man was changing his tune. Finn had stormed out of the senate chambers and returned to his hotel, where he later agreed to speak with a reporter, saying, "[Belvel] is an employee of the senate and I shall certainly have him brought before the bar of the senate for punishment." Taking it one step further, Finn also claimed he would have Belvel "arrested for criminal libel. He must prove his statements." Clearly still enraged, Finn said he would have beaten Belvel "longer and harder, except for the fact that Belvel," according to Finn, "repeatedly said he would take it back" while Finn was in the midst of beating on him. While Belvel was not quite as verbose with the reporter, he did stand by his earlier claim that he was not lying and Finn had truly been found in a house of ill fame.[85]

The next morning, as the senate convened once again, the chamber was filled with an unusual buzz of excitement, and a large crowd had gathered to watch the proceedings, likely hoping for a repeat of the drama from the day before. Not surprisingly, many of Finn's friends in the senate had gathered around his desk and were speaking in hushed tones to one another. When the session was called to order, it was decided that after the very public fight, the senate had no choice but to relieve Belvel of his duties as doorkeeper and to appoint a committee to investigate the charges Belvel had brought against Finn. Ultimately, charges were also brought against Belvel for his slanderous statements against Senator Finn. Whether or not Finn truly was found in a house of ill fame in February 1892, Belvel was not entirely wrong; several years later, police raided that same house of ill fame and found several legislators in residence, whom they quickly placed under arrest.[86]

Managing Vice and Reform Efforts

For a time, citizens of Des Moines considered tolerating the evils of prostitution in the hopes that maybe some good could come from it. Throughout the later part of the nineteenth century, the city council of Des Moines looked to enact various ordinances that would fine and restrict prostitutes and owners of houses of ill fame. Ordinance 4015, issued in 1880, held property owners responsible for operating houses of ill fame and resulted in eight raids on various properties across the city just in the month of December of that year. A proposed ordinance in 1893 called for the issuance of fines to both property owners and prostitutes alike; these fines would range from $50 to $100 and place the offenders in jail for thirty days. In 1893, Alderman Shankland voted for the passage of the ordinance because "he thought the city should derive some revenue from the joints and thought the proposed ordinance would bring into the city treasury a revenue that was now being lost."[87] Not only would these fines bring in funds that could be used to improve the city, but they would also help clean up the streets, albeit temporarily. Since offenders would be imprisoned for a month, the citizens of Des Moines could at least enjoy a brief reprieve from their rowdy neighbors.

There certainly was a profit to be made off the prostitutes, pimps and madams of the city. In April 1900, the police courts reported that they had brought in $600 in fines assessed to those found in disorderly houses. While this was certainly a hefty sum, it did not break the record from one particularly profitable month three years earlier in 1897 when the city had led a massive campaign against the brothels in town that resulted in fines amounting to $800. When one considers that the fines assessed to women found in houses of ill fame in 1900 ranged between $5 and $10, it is hard to believe that the city was not overrun with prostitutes. That being said, the police court did acknowledge that some months were worse than others, considering it had only brought in just over $20 in fines the month before.[88]

While the city claimed that these fines were part of a plan for "making war on the disorderly houses," it is hard to ignore the hypocritical nature of condemning prostitution while also profiting off of it. Certain citizens throughout Des Moines certainly believed so and took it upon themselves to try to reform the fallen women of the city. One particularly successful citizen-led reform society was the Sunbeam Mission. Opening its doors in December 1893, the mission's intent was to aid the unemployed and homeless men of the city. By 1895, the founders of the Sunbeam Mission had reevaluated their initial intent and determined that the fallen women were in far greater need of their help. In order to aid these women, the Sunbeam Mission opened its women's department, which it named the Door of Hope. Those who worked at the Door of Hope believed that all these fallen women in Des Moines needed to turn their lives around was a loving and supportive home to teach them the value of honest work. They offered them a place to stay and provided these women with education, love and support that they believed was so desperately lacking from their lives. When the members of the mission believed that a woman was truly reformed, however long that might take, they made every effort to remove her from the city. Believing that it was the temptations of the capital that had led these women astray in the first place, the members at the mission tried to repair relationships between daughters and their parents, or in cases where these relationships were beyond repair, those at the mission attempted to find another good home for the reformed women outside the city. In order to recruit women to its reform society, the mission used a variety of outreach efforts, including riding through the red-light districts in its gospel wagon singing songs and handing out fliers. The head of the

Sunbeam Rescue Mission

212 WALNUT STREET.

This Ticket Entitles Bearer to sufficient employment to earn Food and Lodgings and Clothing, such as the Mission affords. EVERYONE who will not obey rules and show a disposition to help themselves will forfeit all privileges. MEDICAL ATTENDANCE FREE. CALLS MADE BY MISSIONARIES DAY OR NIGHT.

..............................Name..................St. No.

A ticket that reformers from the Sunbeam Mission handed out to fallen women. *Courtesy Hope Mitchell.*

mission, Frank L. Cramer, was even known to invade brothels when he heard word of a young fallen woman in need of help.[89]

Even though the Sunbeam Mission was located at 212 Walnut on the west side, the superintendent of the Sunbeam Mission, Cramer, was an active advocate for cleaning up the city and aiding the fallen women of Des Moines. In February 1898, he publicly chastised the mayor for claiming that there were no more than thirty houses of ill fame in the city. Cramer challenged the mayor to accompany him on a tour of the city, saying, "I will show him more than thirty places of bad character on the East Side alone." The Sunbeam Mission was located in the western half of the city, but the mission made its best effort to help women throughout the city.[90]

The profits from the fines might have been nice for the city as a whole, but east side citizens and business leaders were quickly tiring of their rowdy neighbors on Court Avenue. Between all the saloons and dens of ill repute, there were some legitimate businesses that had been operating on Court Avenue long before it became the east side red-light district. Many of these businesses employed women to work in their offices, and business owners worried that these women had to endure "insulting remarks and witness disgusting sights as they went to and from their work." In one particularly nasty incident, a young woman was walking home from work around four o'clock in the afternoon when a "drunken wretch…staggered out of a saloon as she was passing. He attempted to put his arms around the girl and drag her from the street." Thankfully, the young woman was able to throw off the man. Instances like these were particularly troubling to the business owners and citizens of East Des Moines who worried they would be seen as "a serious detriment to the East Side as no one from the West Side cares to cross through the vicious atmosphere in order to reach the business district."[91]

While citizen-led reform societies were helpful in addressing the prostitution problem in Des Moines, as the city transitioned into the early twentieth century, east side business leaders began meeting to seriously discuss solutions to the prostitution problem in East Des Moines. It was around this time that the city began cleaning up the other seedy neighborhoods around Des Moines. As a result, many of the displaced women of ill fame began taking up residence on East Court Avenue, and the street was quickly gaining a reputation as "the worst [neighborhood] in Des Moines." By November 1904, the business owners in the area had come up with several solutions. These solutions included circulating a petition among business and property owners that would urge city council to designate police officers to clean up the neighborhood. Another proposed solution focused on attacking the landlords who leased their properties knowing that their tenants would be using them for immoral purposes. East siders were optimistic about this course of action if only for the fact that "instead of fining and prosecuting the women, the rent grabbing landlords should receive the same measure of the law…[and] not let them be shielded by the fines of the women."[92]

Just a month later, in December 1904, East Des Moines business leaders were successful in their efforts to clean up their neighborhood and a case was brought against local landlord Walter Scott. Scott reportedly operated a saloon at 104 East Court Avenue, but he was charged with renting out the apartments above his saloon to prostitutes. Going after the landlords who leased their properties to madams and pimps was not a new technique for cleaning up Des Moines. In 1883, the state had prosecuted landlords W.G. McNulty and Reese Wilkins, who owned properties at 114, 116, 118 and 120 East Court Avenue, and John Lovich, who owned properties in the two hundred block of East Court Avenue. In the 1890s, there was another brief spurt of prosecuting landlords with the case against John Kime for his property at 117 East First Street, just one block south of Court Avenue, in 1892 and J. Gottstein and his property at 416 East Walnut Street in 1895. While charging landlords was a cleanup technique that had been used throughout Des Moines in the past, there was a renewed sense of optimism during the Scott trial, and many believed that Scott's indictment would be the first of many for the disreputable landlords of the city.[93]

As predicted, the case against Walter Scott was the first of many against the unscrupulous landlords of Des Moines. In anticipation of the coming indictments, many west side landlords began cleaning out their properties, claiming, "I did not know that I had any of those kind of places. My agents take care of rental property" and that they were just as anxious to clean up the city as anyone else. The year 1907 saw another slew of indictments; on the east side alone, three landlords were prosecuted for five different properties. These included the T.E. Dowden Company for its property at 118 East Court Avenue, J. Gottstein for his property at 305 East Third Street and Harris Levich for his three properties at 208, 316 and 318 East Court Avenue. While the landlords in the western half of the city could claim ignorance, the landlords of East Des Moines were not so lucky. In the trial against Harris Levich, several of his female tenants testified against him. One of his tenants, Irene Boulding, who rented Levich's property at 208 East Court Avenue, testified that she was renting the ten-room house from Levich to house five girls; during her time in Levich's property, Boulding mentioned that Levich had been to the house to make repairs, making it likely that he had some knowledge of what kind of business she was operating.[94]

East Des Moines business owners were particularly enraged by these irresponsible landlords and worried that their immoral properties would jeopardize their own legitimate businesses. East side business owners and brothers Ben and Sam Cohen were responsible for bringing charges against disreputable landlord J. Gottstein. The Cohen brothers operated an ironworks shop directly across the street from Gottstein's property. With Gottstein's tenants "fighting and raising the devil around there all the time…using profane language and calling name," the brothers worried that Gottstein's business was hurting their own. In the case against T.E. Dowden, Mrs. Eli Cohen and her daughter Sophie operated three businesses in Des Moines, but they were particularly concerned about the prospects for the East Des Moines location at 216 East Third Street after Dowden began to lease his properties to some questionable tenants. Sophie Cohen even confronted Dowden, telling him "he would have to get [his tenants] out," to which Dowden replied that he would not and instead suggested that Sophie and her mother should move their business elsewhere. After charges were brought against Dowden, he tried to play nice with his neighbors, telling Sophie that "if we would drop the charges he would get them out." At the time of the trial, Dowden had moved his tenants, but Sophie was sure that once the trial ended Dowden would "put the same class of people in there."[95]

Aside from fearing for the livelihood of their businesses, East Des Moines citizens feared for the effects that these neighboring houses of ill fame would have on their families, as one concerned citizen voiced to the editor of the *Des Moines Register and Leader* in July 1907:

> *Could any situation be depicted that is more cowardly than this? If our daughters can walk our streets in safety only through the sacrifice of our neighbor's daughter, then our civilization is a failure. Any father or mother who claims that houses of prostitution are a "necessity" let him or her be a loyal citizen and stand ready to sacrifice a daughter for the city's good. When the city of Des Moines takes a revenue from a fallen woman and places her under police protection then the business carried on by her is just as lawful as is that of a grocer to sell sugar or salt. Shame on Des Moines.*[96]

Eradicating Vice

The community-led efforts of targeting the disreputable landlords of the city were effective in undercutting the hold that vice had on various neighborhoods throughout the city, but many credit the massive cleanup of Des Moines' seedier neighborhoods to John L. Hamery. In 1908, the city adopted the Des Moines Plan, which took up the movement the public had already begun at the start of the twentieth century and began a campaign to clean up the red-light districts of the city. Initially, Hamery thought it might be best to simply segregate prostitution to one area within the city, but that idea was met with considerable resistance by east siders.[97]

Rumors began spreading throughout the city about the potential idea of segregating vice to specific neighborhoods in December 1904. When confronted by the *Des Moines Register and Leader*, the police admitted one of their top priorities was finding a solution to the "classes of vice" throughout the city. Segregating vice had been suggested, along with various prospective neighborhoods, but nothing had been decided. The newspaper reported:

> *Some had made the assertion that East Court avenue ought to be put over to this purpose. A wave of protest came from the residents of East Des Moines. The old Whitechapel district has been mentioned. The Italians who own the property declare that they are not sure whether they would agree to it.*[98]

As insubstantial as these rumors might have been, when combined with the cleanup efforts on the west side, the result was an influx of vice into East Des Moines. The *Des Moines Register and Leader* reported that "Court avenue is already crowded with disorderly houses and business men object to that locality being lengthened." Rather than segregating the women of ill fame into any one neighborhood, "what ought to be done by the police is break up every place resorted to for immoral purposes in Des Moines. It can be done. The evil can be reduced to a minimum."[99] Unfortunately for the citizens of Des Moines, that lofty goal was still a few years off.

By 1906, it appeared that segregation seemed to be the best choice for managing the prostitution problem in the city. As the state continued to prosecute the landlords of the city, the *Des Moines Register and Leader* reported that "it is probable that dozens of places will be close, and the remaining ones herded into a definite district, where they can be more easily and thoroughly supervised by the authorities than they have been in the past." When trying to determine where best to house the prostitutes, Hamery took a tour of the city with the chief of police. The men drove down Cherry Street on the west side and then made their way over to the old Whitechapel neighborhood on Pelton Avenue. Finally, the men toured East Court Avenue, exploring First Street through Fourth Street. At the end of the tour, it was determined that the red-light district in East Des Moines was far and away the worst in the city at that point in time, and Chief Jones openly remarked, "I don't blame the west side women for not wanting to come over here." Even with that in mind, Hamery wondered if perhaps it might be best to segregate Des Moines' prostitutes to the south of the city so as to keep them out of the way of the rest of the citizens.[100]

By 1908, Hamery had had a change of heart and determined that segregating vice to one neighborhood within the city was no solution at all. As he would say in his 1909 book, *War on the White Slave Trade*:

> *Segregation as applied to prostitutes is but another term for incubation; that it is the nucleus and back bone of the white slave trade; that segregation is affiliated with gambling, boot-legging, opium and cocaine dives and other vices; that it forms an education for school children in vice when they may pass down a street on the way to and from school.*[101]

In order to push prostitution out of the city, Hamery approved a massive citywide arrest of prostitutes in late August 1908. When word spread about Hamery's plans, many of the city's prostitutes decided to hedge their bets and left town before Hamery had a chance to throw them in jail, heading to larger cities in the Midwest like St. Louis, Chicago and Minneapolis. A reporter from the *Iowa State Register* did a tour of East Court Avenue the night before Hamery's rumored string of arrests and noted that that night "saw many darkened houses on East Court avenue and East Second street." The same reporter optimistically declared that his tour "through Des Moines' red light district last night showed conclusively that the social evil in Des Moines has received a death blow." While the women who could afford to leave the city had certainly done so, sadly, there were "dozens of penniless girls" who could not scrimp together the money to escape Des Moines' abandoned red-light district. In order to aid these women, Hamery enlisted the aid of the humane society and other charitable organizations in the city to care for these desolate women who had been left behind.[102]

While Hamery was likely unable to banish vice from the city entirely, he did make a tremendous step toward dramatically cleaning up the city. His work helped to better the reputation of the city, and as claimed by the *Des Moines Tribune-Capital*, "the capital of Iowa is held up before America…as a model city of moral cleanliness." By the 1920s and 1930s, the results of Hamery's efforts could still be seen throughout the former red-light districts of Des Moines. By 1922, some citizens were complaining about the run-down condition of the old Whitechapel neighborhood in the western half of the city. After the evacuation of the prostitutes and other dens of vice, the neighborhood had been taken over by some of the poorest families in the city. In 1928, the city building commissioner declared many of the buildings unfit for residence. Unfortunately, the city had the difficult task of tracing the ownership of all the old dens of ill repute before it could proceed with demolition. Apparently, these efforts were successful because by 1931, the city had began work on demolishing twenty to thirty of the dilapidated tenements buildings in old Whitechapel.[103]

Demolishing the old red-light districts certainly helped to clean up the city, but as Des Moines moved into the Great Depression, some citizens reminisced about the carefree lifestyle of days past. Prior to the imminent demolition of Whitechapel, several local newspapers ran a series of articles detailing the history of Des Moines' old red-light districts. In 1929, the *Des Moines Tribune-Capital* interviewed longtime East Des Moines resident Jerry Gardineer, who had lived in the neighborhood for forty years. East Des Moines had once been home to thirty-five saloons and had a string of "red lights [that] dotted Court avenue from the river to East Sixth street." Now, this block featured fading advertisements that read, "Drink Old Tavern

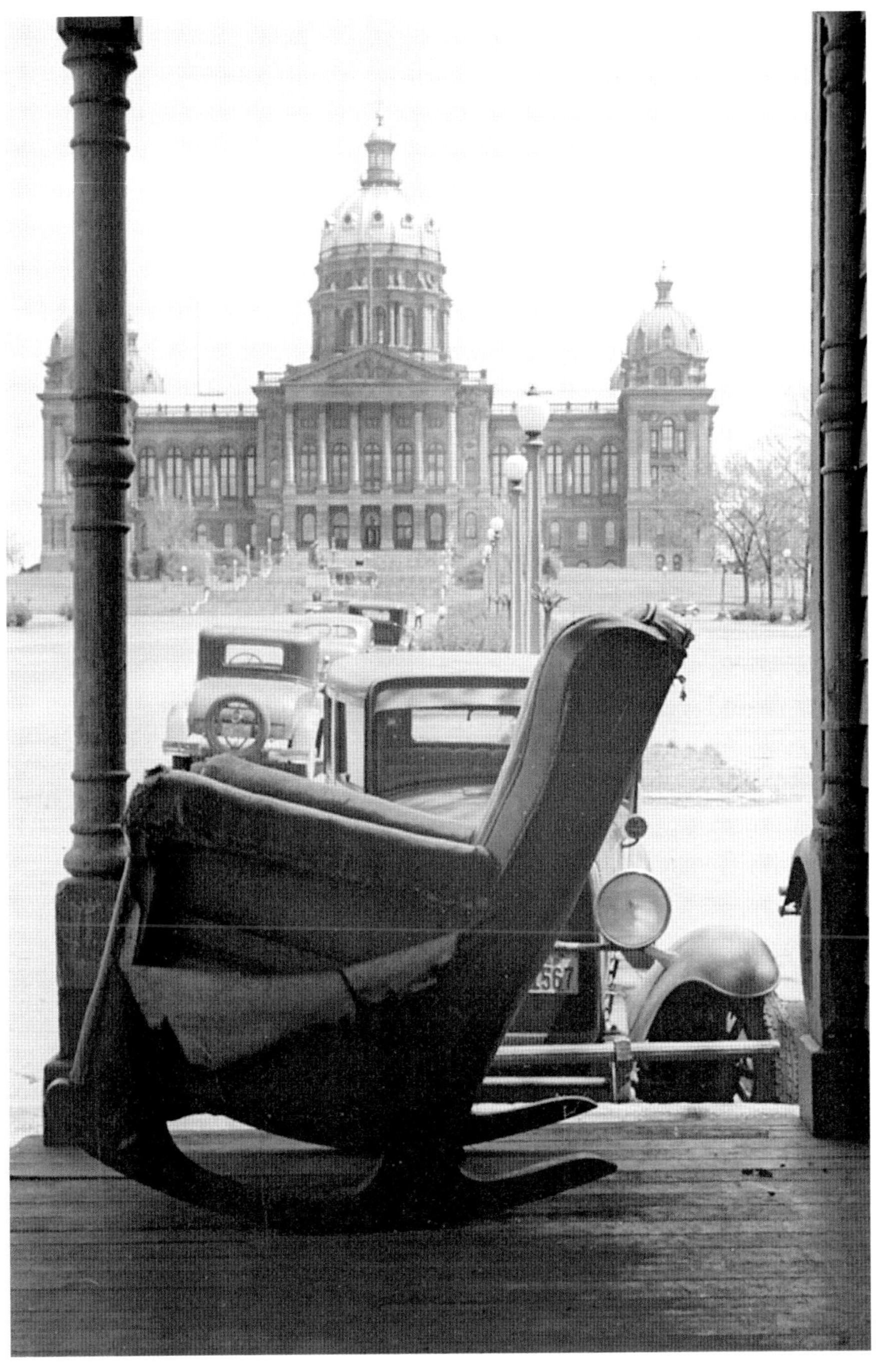

A photo showcasing the contrasting neighborhoods surrounding the capitol. *Library of Congress, Prints & Photographs Division, FSA/OWI Collection LC-USF33-T01-001867.*

Beer. Made in Des Moines," painted along the walls of old saloons that housed quiet pool halls and drugstores. Gardineer fondly recalled the hustle and bustle of the old red-light neighborhood. "Business went on twenty four hours a day. Drunken brawls and fist fights went on every day, but few men carried a gun," he recalled whimsically of the rough-and-tumble neighborhood. But after the red-light districts across the city had been cleaned out in the early twentieth century, the city quickly took over what might have been considered historic locations of vice in Des Moines. According to Gardineer, the "first east side saloon stood where the new federal building now stands" at the corner of East First Street and East Walnut; another saloon stood at the site of the new city hall in East Des Moines, and one had even been located across the street from where the new police station stood. While longtime residents like Gardineer might have missed the culture of their old neighborhood, there was no arguing that cleaning up the neighborhood had greatly improved the safety of East Des Moines. After the closing of the red-light districts throughout the city, Hamery reported that the city saw a dramatic drop in crime, stating that "there was less crime in the eighteen months following the closing of the district than there was in the six months preceding."[104]

Despite Hamery's efforts to clean up the red-light districts and municipal efforts to take over the sites of notorious saloons across the city, it would be naïve to believe that vice had been completely eradicated from Des Moines. In the 1920s, a small syndicate of prostitution moved onto Des Moines Street between East Second and Third until the police eventually raided the block in 1929. In the decades that followed, prostitution still held a small foothold in the east side in East Fourth Street and Locust, where it was rumored that women rented out rooms above the bar called Betty's Place for less than respectable purposes. Even though vice was never truly eradicated from the city, much of the progress in cleaning up East Des Moines was made possible by the active and concerned business owners in the area who wished to see the eastern half of the city thrive rather than drown in the vice of Court Avenue.[105]

Chapter 5

Building Up the East Side Business

About the same time that vice was making its way to East Court Avenue, just a few blocks away on East Locust, many other citizens of East Des Moines were also embracing their entrepreneurial spirit. Throughout the later part of the nineteenth century, the east side began to develop a business district that would rival its counterpart in the western half of the city. While the business district in East Des Moines would never truly be able to compete with that in the western half of the city in size or stature, these business owners played a tremendous role not only in shaping the East Village as we know it today but also in serving and cleaning up the community.

The Hohberger Building

The late nineteenth century saw a real estate boom in East Des Moines, and on January 1, 1878, the *Iowa State Register* observed that "the East Side has added very largely to its buildings, and of a most substantial character." Leading the charge on this east side renovation was John Hohberger, who began construction on what would eventually become an east side gem. Hohberger invested $3,500 in the construction of a three-story brick structure. Measuring in at twenty feet by sixty feet, the building was part of what would become a larger business block on the fifth block of East Locust.[106] On December 12, 1878, the *Leader* noted the following:

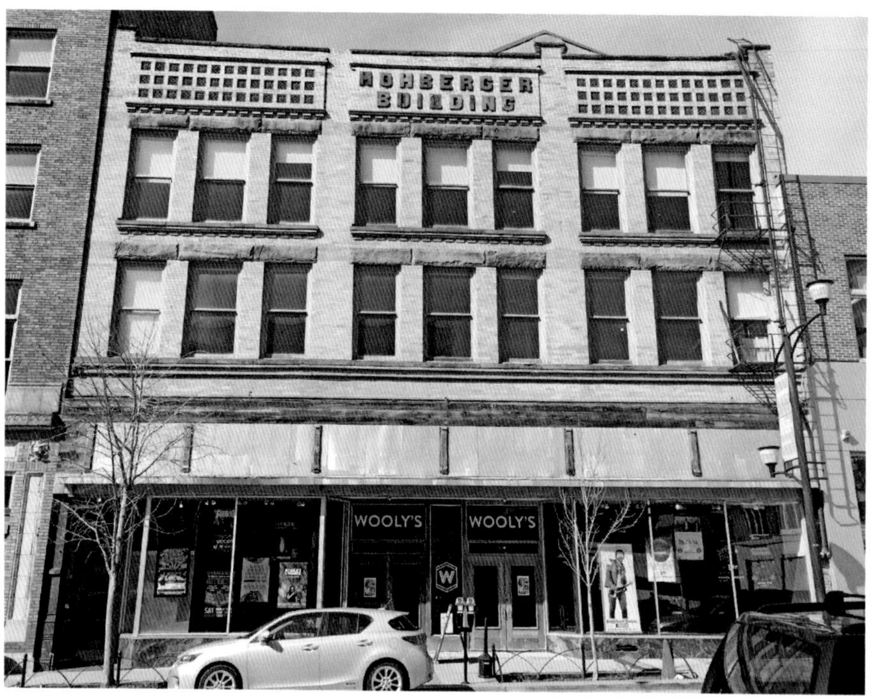

The Hohberger Building as it stands today. *Courtesy Hope Mitchell.*

> *On the East Side Mr. Hoberger* [sic] *and Mr. Fairall have reared exceptional business blocks which are to the credit of themselves and every dweller on that side of the river. A curious feature of the business building is that it has all been done up on the theory that trade is moving away from the river. The same stores on the river bank would lie idle and the probability is that the move is a discerning one.*[107]

When Des Moines was founded, much of the business had, for obvious reason, developed around the fort, which had been constructed along the western bank of the Des Moines River. As the city continued to grow and develop, it made sense that business would eventually move inland to a more central location to better serve the surrounding population on the east side of the river. Additionally, less reputable businesses tended to congregate around the river, so it would only make sense that many business owners wished to distance themselves from their less reputable counterparts. This was an accurate prediction on the part of the *Leader*, as business continued to move inland on the east side. In July 1880, the *Register* reported, "The East Side is showing every sign of life and prosperity. All its business men are doing well, and new business houses are being added weekly. The work of improvement over there this year is remarkable, both in the business and residence parts of town."[108]

Where Hohberger had begun construction just a year and a half beforehand, there were now seven storefronts under construction on Locust by other prominent businessmen in the community, including George Garver, H.E. Teachout, W.V. Williams and E.J. Fairall.[109] By this time, Hohberger was the proprietor of both 506 and 508 Locust and the building had almost doubled in size, now measuring forty-four by eighty feet. One of the first tenants in Hohberger's new building was the Hollingsworth & Jones agricultural implements dealership. Hollingsworth & Jones opened its doors in 1878 and very quickly became a shining example of commercial success on the east side of the city. With all its newfound success, Hollingsworth & Jones needed to rent out all of Hohberger's new building, which included three floors and the basement.[110]

By 1883, Hollingsworth & Jones had taken its business elsewhere, and it was rumored that the new American Savings Bank would take up residence in the Hohberger Building in November of that year. The American Savings Bank had considered various locations on both the east and west sides of the river, but what ultimately convinced it to bring its business to East Des Moines was the rapid rate of growth it witnessed in that half of the city. The west side had an assessed property value of $6,299,309 and the east side of $2,270,575, but the east side had a growth rate of 70 percent from the prior year.[111] Granted, this was the opinion of a east side–based newspaper, so the decision may have been as simple as the rents on the east side were cheaper, but either way, the addition of the American Savings Bank in a location that was central to all east siders was of great benefit to the surrounding community. By 1887, the Hohberger Block was the banking center of East Des Moines, as it was now home to two banks; the American Savings Bank was still on the ground floor, and the Capital City Bank, a subsidiary of the Des Moines Loan & Trust Company, also moved into the Hohberger block.[112]

Over the coming years, the Hohberger Block continued to be a desirable location for successful east side businesses. In 1895, the building was expanded to include the neighboring location of 504 Locust. The addition cost $45,000, and the expanded building was the new how to the Dockstader & Wilkins Fair Store.[113] C.B. Dockstader was born in Pennsylvania in 1844 and made his way to Iowa in 1856. After serving in the Civil War, he returned to Iowa, where he farmed and ran a hardware store in Panora until 1882. After gaining some experience managing a hardware store, Dockstader purchased an interest in the Barnett & Wilkins dry good company, which he eventually renamed Dockstader & Wilkins. By 1900, Dockstader was the sole owner and renamed the business C.B. Dockstader Company to reflect these changes. By 1907, Dockstader was able to incorporate the business with capital stock of $40,000.[114] The Fair Store was the largest dry goods establishment and was one of the premier businesses on the east side at the time. The Fair Store occupied the first floor and basement of the Hohberger Block. In order to better accommodate their business, Dockstader and Wilkins renovated their storefront and added a $6,000 soda fountain. The Fair Store happily made its home in the Hohberger Block until it was eventually bought out by Mandelbaums in 1918.[115]

Aside from acting as a home to some of the most affluent businesses on the east side, the Hohberger Block also hosted various community-driven functions. Throughout the nineteenth century, the Vasa Literary Society and the Hanskrygerraminde Danish Library both met at Hohbergers.[116] Additionally, Hohbergers also offered a temporary home to the Jewish population of East Des Moines when the B'nai Israel Children of Israel group, founded in 1876, needed a meeting place. The group used the Hohberger Building as its temporary meeting place until a synagogue was eventually constructed.[117] Today, the Hohberger Building is home to one of the East Village's premier concert venues, Wooly's.

Capital City State Bank

While a number of banks made their homes on the east side of downtown Des Moines, the Capital City State Bank holds a special place in East Des Moines history because of the role it played in shaping the landscape of east downtown Des Moines and the bank's ability to withstand a series of severe financial depressions that spanned the nation. Originally founded in 1869 by B.F. Allen and A.L. West, the bank quickly changed hands when it was sold to William Christy and Isaac Brandt. The Capital City Bank experienced a serious rough patch when it refused to cash two overdrafts, which reduced its funds from $9,000 to $4,000. After that, the bank temporarily closed its doors until it was reorganized and reopened in August 5, 1878. In the reorganization, Christy stayed on as cashier, while A.W. Naylor took over as president with William Haskell serving as vice-president. In order to prevent any repeats of the overdraft fiasco, the newly reorganized bank adopted a resolution that prohibited overdrafts and put a $10,000 limit on loans.[118]

The Capital City State Bank was able to weather the panic of the 1890s, although the panic did result in a drop in deposits from $377,676 to $300,538 from 1893 to 1894. By 1896, the decline had continued, with deposits hitting a low of $263,607. With a slight spike in its 1898 deposits to $279,682, Capital City State Bank was feeling optimistic, sharing the following in its annual minutes:[119] "Few institutions have had so many odds to contend with and have come through with a better showing. With the experience of the past to guide us and better times before us we cannot but feel that prosperity and success such as have not hitherto been known lie before us."[120]

Indeed, better times certainly were ahead for the members of Capital City State Bank. At the turn of the twentieth century, the bank was able to absorb the American Savings Bank and absorbed 95 percent of its clientele. As a result, by January 1900, deposits were up to $557,283 and had almost doubled to $931,712 by the next year. In response to this dramatic and sudden growth, the Capital City State Bank began considering expanding its business into a newer and larger building, and in 1901, a building committee was formed. Interestingly, when the committee began searching for potential lots, it considered purchasing the lot of the former American Savings Bank, which would eventually become the site of the Teachout Building. Eventually, the committee settled on a lot on the opposite side of East Locust and determined that it wanted to build the east side's first skyscraper; the building was slated to be seven stories high and cost approximately $100,000. Construction was completed on East Des Moines' first skyscraper in 1903, and Capital City State Bank reopened its doors on May 26. In addition to housing the bank, the new Capital City State Bank skyscraper was also home to several other prominent east side businesses, including the *Daily Tribune* newspaper.[121] Ultimately, the construction of the Capital City State Bank skyscraper did much to set the tone for the east side, as the *Tribune* noted:

> *East Locust street, between Fourth and Sixth streets, is the great center of business. The erection of the seven-story brick building by the Capital City State Bank, at the corner of Fifth and Locust streets, has firmly anchored the center of business in East Des Moines for the present, or until some enterprising man erects a greater building.*[122]

Throughout the twentieth century, the Capital City State Bank continued to grow and expand, so much so that in 1910, F.M. Hubbell attempted to merge Capital City State Bank with the East Side Home Savings Bank. Hubbell was a big player on the west side of the river, and in order to merge the two banks, he attempted to gain control of Capital City State Bank by purchasing a majority of its shares. By December 1910, Hubbell owned 509 shares, but unfortunately, that was just over a third of the total shares; with no sign that he would be able to obtain a controlling interest, Hubbell sold his shares on December 10. While the bank survived the Great Depression, the other remaining east side bank, the Home Savings Bank, went under. Capital City State Bank was able to absorb Home Savings on March 4, 1938, but this now meant that there was only one bank on the east side of the river. By the 1950s, Capital City State Bank's holdings amounted to $75 million. It also continued to expand by purchasing several buildings along East Fifth Street, just to the south of the bank, and demolishing them in order to create parking and a drive-through teller for customers. In 1980, the Hawkeye Bancorporation purchased the bank, and it then went through a series of name changes and successful mergers with other banks. Unfortunately, the Capital City State Bank skyscraper did not have a similarly successful fate; by 1981, it was determined that the seven-story building was beyond repair, and it was demolished.[123]

The Teachout Building

For a time, the Capital City State Bank Building was the only skyscraper on the east side—that is, until the Teachout Building came along just a few years later.[124] While a majority of Des Moines' skyscrapers were located on the west side of the city, the construction of the Teachout Building, built between 1911 and 1912, was the east side's attempt to keep pace with much of the west side development. Horace E. Teachout made his way from New York to the east side of Des Moines in 1876 and quickly became a prominent and well-respected member of the community. In 1880, he was appointed by Governor Merrill to the Des Moines Improvement Committee and was elected as secretary of the chamber of commerce. Teachout was an incredibly busy man with his hands in many businesses throughout the city. Prior to constructing his namesake building, he also had his hands in developing the first electric streetcar system in Des Moines between 1886 and 1888, which he was able to sell to Jefferson Polk for $350,000 just one year after he completed construction. While Teachout appreciated construction and building up the public transportation system throughout Des Moines, his primary business was in ice; he was the founder of both the

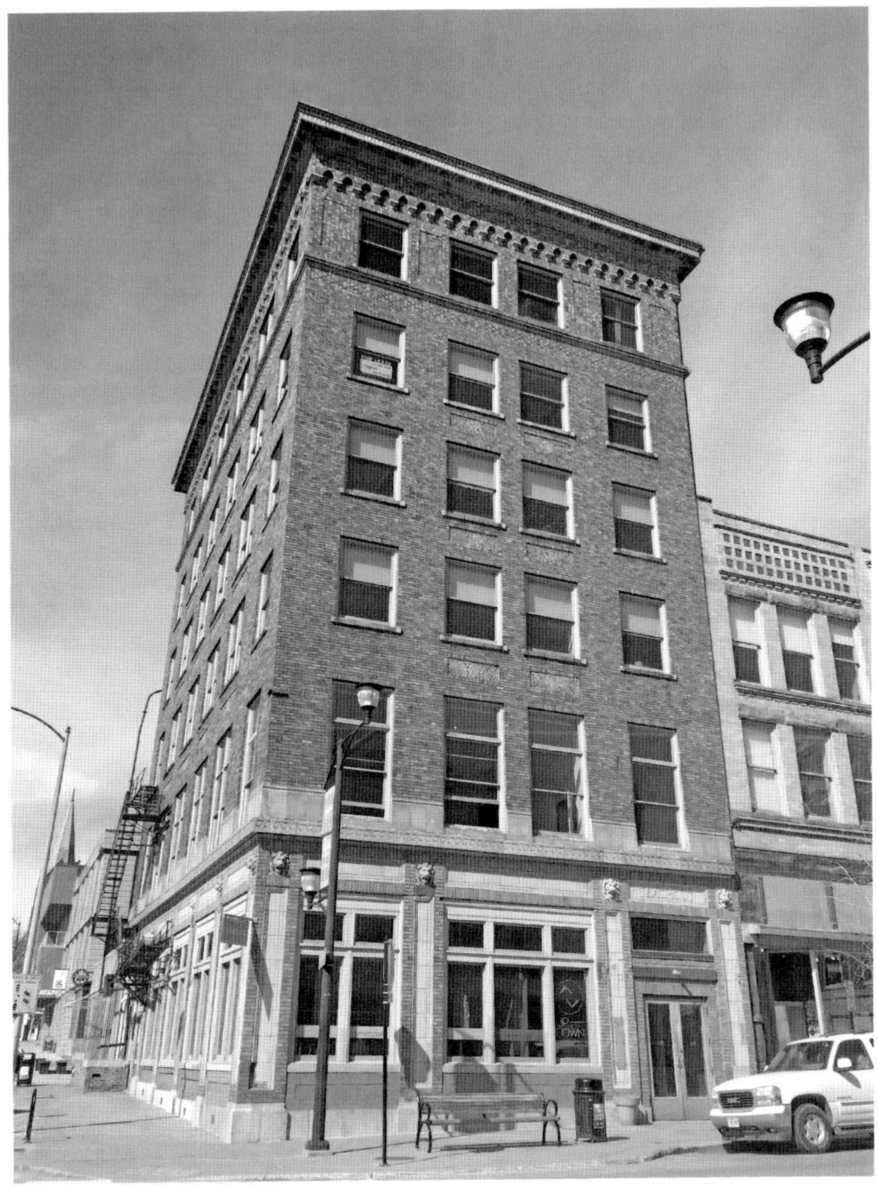

The Teachout Building as it stands today. *Courtesy Hope Mitchell.*

Capital City Ice Company and the Des Moines Ice Company. Additionally, he assisted in developing the Mutual Telephone Company in 1889 and the Home Savings Bank and also served as vice-president at five other banks across the state. In 1895, Teachout continued in his legacy of civil service to the city of Des Moines when he was elected as county supervisor. He then became the chairman and served until 1899. Shortly after taking his seat as the county supervisor, Teachout also began serving on the East Des Moines School Board in 1896 and acted as treasurer until 1900. And finally, to round out his service to the city of Des Moines and the state as a whole, Teachout also acted as a Republican representative in the Twenty-ninth through Thirty-first General Assemblies, beginning in 1901. Sadly, Teachout's personal residence at 1301 East Grand Avenue was demolished in the creation of I-235 in 1966.[125]

While Teachout was clearly an active and devoted east sider with a tremendous number of contributions to the city of Des Moines and state of Iowa, arguably his most enduring contribution would be his namesake, the Teachout Building. While the east side of Des Moines never was truly able to compete with the west side when it came to skyscrapers, the Teachout Building was still a sign of hope and prosperity to those invested in the commercial well-being of East Des Moines. As noted earlier, Teachout was heavily involved in the construction and development of Des Moines. In 1880, the east side newspaper *Plain Talk* reported that Teachout and one of his partners, Fairall, had opened a new hall on the east that was fast "becoming very popular for social gatherings and its owners are likely to be well paid for their foresight in putting up a hall of this kind," but it is unclear whether this gathering hall was the location of the future Teachout Building.[126] In all likelihood, this was the location of the future Teachout skyscraper, as in that same year, Teachout was also recognized along with Fairall for building up the business district of the east side on Locust. Unfortunately, all this development required a bit of demolition. The construction on the fifth block of Locust meant that the 1854 residence of Dr. Courtney, who had once been known as the "social prince" around early Des Moines, and a grand old oak tree behind Courtney's home had to be removed. While many regretted the loss, the *Register* summed it nicely, stating, "But so it goes, in making a city."[127] Near the end of that same decade, Teachout's property at 500 East Locust, which would eventually become home to the six-story east side skyscraper, expanded to twenty-two by seventy-five feet and was home to the American Savings Bank.[128]

As East Des Moines began to settle into the twentieth century, there was a growing desire for larger office space. In 1909, the east side Commercial

Club took note of the fact that the only real large office space available for east side businesses was in the Capital City State Bank Building. The group worried that the east side did not have office space to offer businesses "equal [to] those of the west side" and that this absence might push businesses out of East Des Moines. While these concerns were justified, there was one major hurdle facing east side developers of the early twentieth century. Landownership in the eastern half of downtown Des Moines had always been very fragmented, with many property owners with small lots patchworked together, rather than a few owners controlling all the large tracts of land. In fact, even the largest office space in East Des Moines that the Commercial Club cited, the Capital City State Bank lot, was actually controlled by four individual lot owners. The largest tract of land in east downtown under single ownership was actually the Hohberger Building, which in 1909 was home to the Iowa Trust & Savings Bank, the Mitchell Pharmacy and still housed the Fair Store. As they approached the end of the first decade of the twentieth century, East Des Moines business leaders began seeking out prime locations in the downtown area for future expansion, including the construction of a three-story department store and larger downtown office space. In their search, they considered three primary locations along Locust, with the northeast corner of Locust and East Fifth being of particular interest to various parties. Either way, all parties agreed that this would be a considerable project, as all the prospective locations would require demolition of existing structures.[129]

The Commercial Club's focus on Locust and East Fifth was no accident. Since the latter part of the nineteenth century, Locust had grown to become the commercial epicenter of the east side. Meanwhile, East Fifth was widely regarded as a prime location for banking, retail stores and theaters on the east side. After the construction of the east side's first skyscraper, the Capital City State Bank Building in 1903, the fifth block of East Locust was declared by the east side newspaper *Plain Talk* to be "firmly anchored [as] the center of business" in East Des Moines. Locating the east side's second skyscraper, which was intended to house much-needed office space for east side businesses, in the center of much of the east side's business, entertainment and shopping district was the most desirable option for east side developers.[130]

By 1911, the Commercial Club had settled on the location of the east side's second skyscraper at its desired location on the northeast corner of Locust and East Fifth. Horace Teachout owned the lot; when he had originally purchased it in 1894, it was home to a two-story building that

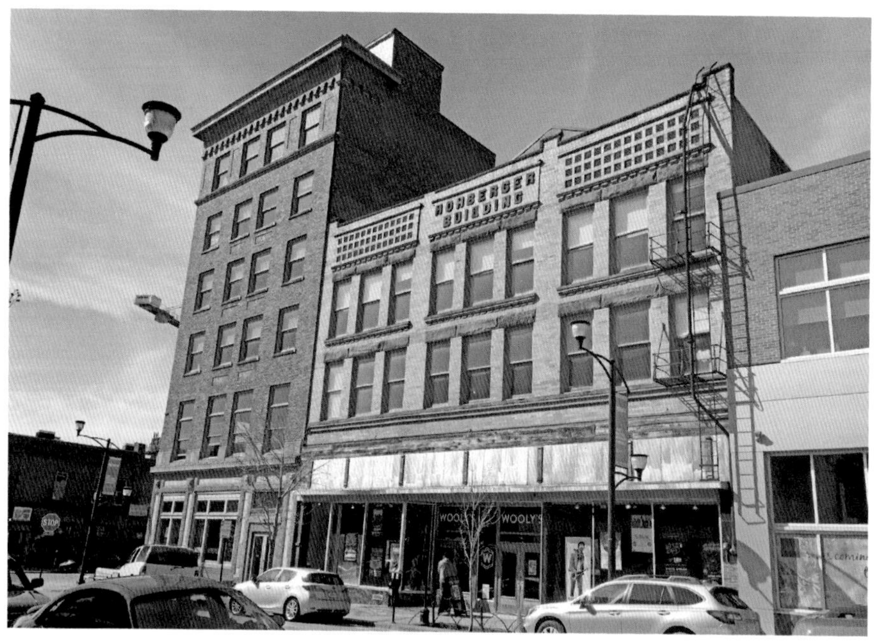

The Teachout and Hohberger Buildings as they stand today. *Courtesy Hope Mitchell.*

housed the Leader Clothing Store on the ground floor and the Iowa Trust & Savings Bank on the second floor. Architects Proudfoot, Bird & Rawson took on the task of designing the east side's newest skyscraper. In developing their designs, the architects took into account several factors, including the fact that this new skyscraper would be located just across the street from the east side's until then sole skyscraper, the Capital City State Bank Building, and that this new construction represented a major resurgence of commercial growth and development on the east side of Des Moines. In order to ensure that this new skyscraper complemented the current Capital City State Bank Building, the architects determined that this new skyscraper's scale should be comparable. Initially, they decided that the future skyscraper would be six stories tall, but midway through the construction, Teachout began to second-guess this decision and wanted to add a final seventh story to his namesake structure in order to compete with the Capital City State Bank Building. Unfortunately, that final story was never added, and the Teachout Building was destined to remain just slightly shorter than its neighbor, the Capital City State Bank.[131]

The construction of the Teachout Building was filled with its fair share of hurdles. In addition to the second-guessing that occurred in regard to the height of the building, the architects of the Teachout Building needed to contend with the challenges that came with the less than ideal lot shape; in fact, the lot sizes created so many hurdles that Teachout worried he was only going to lose money on this building. As mentioned earlier, a challenge to east side development was the small lot sizes. While the site for the Teachout Building was the single largest parcel of land held by one owner, the lot was still quite narrow in comparison to lots used for skyscrapers on the west side. As a result, the Teachout Building had to assume a very narrow rectangular shape. Since the building was so narrow, that meant that a large proportion of square footage was devoted to the stairwell and elevator. Finally, the builders had to contend with how to handle the rear of the building. Being that buildings on the east side of the river generally capped off at about three stories, they often backed up to one another, and builders therefore did not have to worry about the appearance of the exterior of the back of their buildings. While this may have been a concern for the Capital City State Bank Building, it had not been a pressing issue, as the façade of the building faced the capitol with the rear of the building facing away from the city center. Since the new Teachout Building was on the northeast corner of Locust and East Fifth, that meant that the rear of the building would be facing the state capitol and the rest of the east side city center. Initially, it appears that the builders wrapped the brick from the façade of the building around half of the northern wall, but for some reason—perhaps budget was an issue—the brick was only added to half the wall. As a solution to disguise the unsightly rear of the new East Des Moines skyscraper, the owners painted large advertisements on the back of building; as a result, the Capital City State Bank also adopted this method of beautifying the rear of its building.[132]

After completion in 1912, the Teachout provided office space for various east side professionals, including Steward & Hextell law office, Jno T. Christie's insurance office, the Union Realty Company and a number of physicians. Several years after its completion, the top floor of the Teachout Building was renovated to include a suite of rooms for the East Des Moines Commercial Club; aside from those changes, the Teachout Building remained fairly untouched and continued to serve as home to various other East Des Moines–based businesses over the coming years. While the Teachout Building was a major accomplishment for east side business leaders, in many ways it was also an end of sorts. Business would obviously continue to grow and develop throughout the east side, but in many ways, the Teachout Building was the final attempt to bring large-scale office space

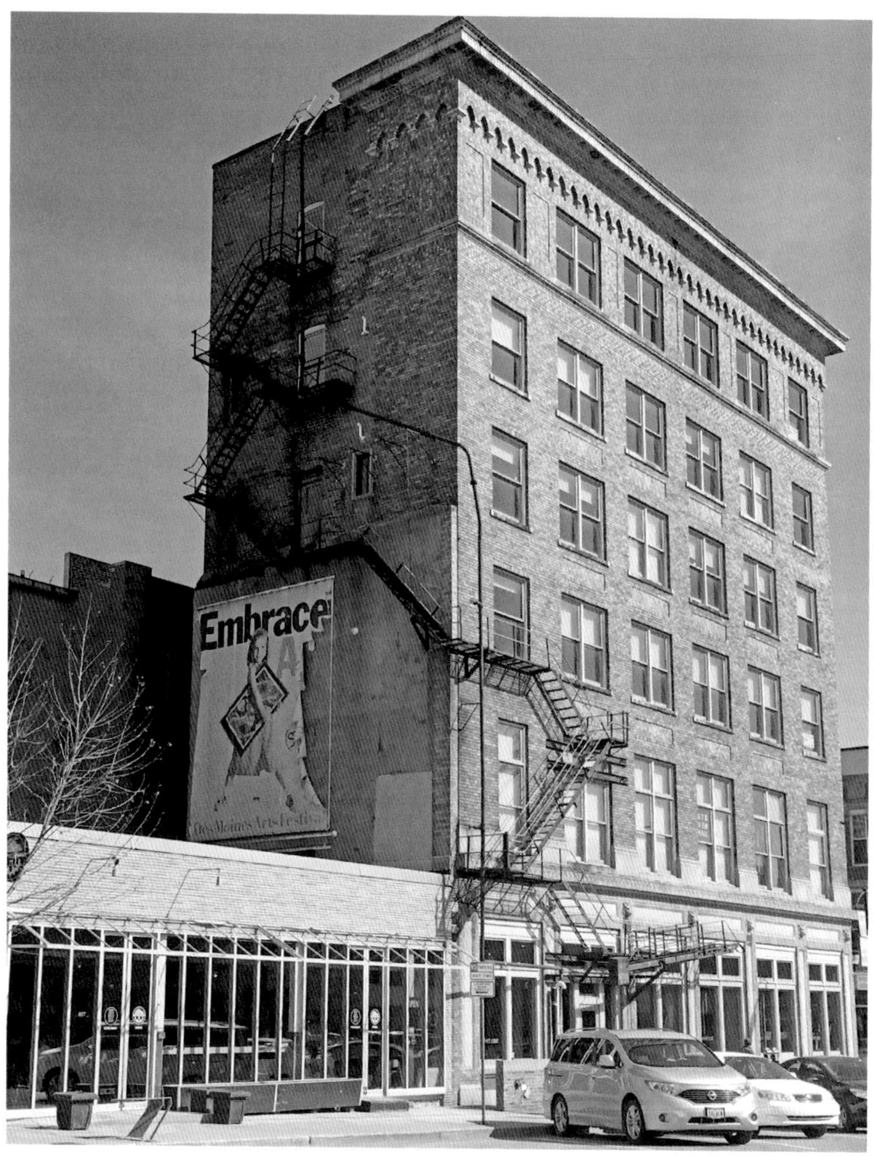

Even today, advertisements are used to cover the unsightly rear of the Teachout Building. *Courtesy Hope Mitchell.*

to the east side. While government-funded construction of this scale would succeed later in the century, no projects of Teachout's size or scale would take off on the east side until the twenty-first century.[133]

THE LEWIS OPERA HOUSE

A major cultural institution of the early east side was the Lewis Opera House, built by Charles G. Lewis in 1877. Lewis was an interesting east side character. On the one hand, he was a prominent figure in the community; aside from building the opera house, he also served as deputy county treasurer and then went on to serve as the county treasurer. Due to both financial and some rather scandalous personal troubles, Lewis had to leave Des Moines for a time but returned to the city around 1901 to live out his remaining years. After his death in 1903, Lewis was still causing a stir when a formerly unknown wife from Buffalo, New York, arrived in Des Moines to lay claim to his remaining estate.[134]

For an establishment that would be in the spotlight of East Des Moines' entertainment scene, the Lewis Opera House made a very subdued entrance to East Des Moines. Unfortunately, a lack of an east side–based newspaper at the time meant a lack of coverage on the development of the opera house, but a west side newspaper, the *Leader*, did cover some of the highlights. Construction on the opera house began in the spring of 1877 between Fifth and Sixth Streets on Locust and ultimately cost Lewis $30,000. By May, the crew had finished excavating the lot and laying the foundation. By July, the construction team was installing "massive iron fronts," and the *Leader* admired that this now gave the street a more "cosmopolitan appearance." As with its beginning, the Lewis Opera House again made a very quiet debut in East Des Moines when it was simply announced in late September 1877 that the Lee Township Democrats had reserved the new opera house for their next meeting.[135]

After its rather demure introduction, the Lewis Opera House began to recruit more high-end events as it settled into its first year of business. On January 17, 1878, the Swedish Quintette club performed for the formal opening of the opera house. A few weeks later, Governor John H. Gear and Lieutenant Governor Frank T. Campbell held their inauguration at the newly constructed opera house.[136] The opera house continued to gain clout, as *Plain Talk* proclaimed that the "most brilliant social event" to ever take place at the Lewis Opera House was held in February 1879 in celebration of the fourth anniversary of the Capital Lodge. The celebration was described as follows:

> *The house was crowded with the best people of the east city, and many from the west side. The parquet was cleared of its seats, which were then*

moveable chairs, and dancing was indulged in by old and young—some of the former not having indulged in anything of the kind for a score or more of years. The state was filled with tables loaded with food, presented a very picturesque appearance.[137]

Unfortunately, Lewis's success with the opera house was short-lived. In 1881, he began experiencing some financial difficulties and was forced to declare bankruptcy. Much of Lewis's financial trouble actually began before the opera house was even complete. During the construction process, he had found that the costs were "largely more than [he had] anticipated," and ultimately, he had to take out $5,000 in mechanics' liens. Lewis made a deal of sorts with local businessman John M. Day, who took over running the opera house through 1878. As time went on, the opera house was not quite as profitable as had been expected, and Lewis's financial troubles thereby worsened. He tried to pass responsibility for the building onto Day, but the courts ultimately decided that Lewis was the owner and therefore responsible for the debt. On September 30, 1881, the opera house was sold at a sheriff's sale to George P. Bissell. Bissell was able to purchase the opera house for $20,000, which was quite the steal, considering Lewis had spent $10,000 more constructing it less than five years earlier. Interestingly, it had been Bissell who loaned Lewis $11,000 in 1877 to build the opera house to begin with.[138]

The change of ownership thankfully did nothing to dampen the opera house's presence and activism in the east side community. The following year, in 1882, *Plain Talk* noted that it was the Lewis Opera House that kicked off the Christmas shopping season in downtown East Des Moines with a balloon ascension for the community.[139] But for all its efforts, the opera house still struggled to entice an audience. In 1885, *Plain Talk* reported the following:

No matter how good a company is billed for the East Side Opera House, or how low the rates of admission, an audience large enough to make it worth the while playing can rarely be obtained.... The citizens of East Des Moines should take pride in supporting an enterprise of this kind as far as they are able, and remember that an opera house helps to form a city as well as anything else.

According to *Plain Talk*, the theater manager had "strained every nerve for the past two or three years" in order to attract new and interesting acts and drum up excitement, but it was all for naught. For example, the Mortimer and

Weaver Dramatic Company had agreed to perform at the opera house. This was quite the find, considering it ranked "among the best in the profession." But even with ticket prices as low as fifteen cents, the attendance was still very small. A *Plain Talk* reporter had some harsh last words for the east siders, saying, "We think this all comes from thoughtlessness on the part of our East Des Moines neighbors and hope that they will awake to the fact that this side of the river should have and sustain at least one opera house."[140] Apparently, the east siders did not awake to that fact, because by 1887 the Capital City Opera House was listed among the city's improvements for the year, and it is believed that this new opera house was simply a remodeled version of the old Lewis Opera House.[141] On the one hand, it may have been concerning that the opera house was changing hands yet again, but in many ways, it was likely a blessing that the east side still had its own opera house.

Unfortunately, the Lewis Opera House was not destined to become an east side landmark. In February 1892, it burned to the ground; thankfully, the fire did not occur in the middle of a performance, and no one was hurt. Over the years, the opera house had grown, and by 1892, the building occupied three lots and was three stories tall. Sadly, the entire structure, including the basement, had to be gutted after the fire. Just two years before the fire, the building had gone into foreclosure and was purchased by the Merchants Savings Bank, based out of Providence, Rhode Island. The bank had then leased the opera house to J.A. Connolley, who had done his best to try to reinvigorate it. He added more seating and steam heating for the patrons, along with various other improvements. Even with all these enhancements, the opera house still struggled to draw an audience; the writers at *Plain Talk* noted that the opera house had been struggling for some time, and "efforts to attract first class performances to the house [had] met with only poor success. Most of the bills presented [had] been of the cheaper kind, and rarely popular at that." Even though the opera house had failed to attract hordes of east siders, the citizens of East Des Moines were sad to see it go. Very soon after the fire, there was discussion of replacing the opera house as soon as July of that year, but by 1895, the opera house had still not been reconstructed.[142]

WATERBURY CHEMICAL COMPANY

While the east side may have lost its only opera house as it approached the twentieth century, that was not necessarily a sign of things to come for business in East Des Moines. In 1898, F.C. Waterbury was working as a drugstore clerk when he developed a cream, which he named the Waterbury Compound, that would launch his career. Waterbury continued to work at the drugstore while selling his compound cream on the side, but as his own business grew, he began looking for a larger and more permanent location in which to produce his compound. Initially, he was based in the western half of downtown Des Moines. The first Waterbury plant was located at West Court Avenue and Fourth Street in what was the former *Des Moines Register* building. From there, Waterbury moved to the GAR building located at Mulberry and Sixth Streets and then built a brand-new plant at Grand Avenue and Ninth Street. After bouncing around the west side of the river, Waterbury decided to explore his options on the east side. He decided on the former Capital Publishing Plant, located at East Locust and Second Street. Waterbury's new location had originally been constructed in 1899 for the newspaper the *Daily Iowa Capital*. This was a strategic move on the part of the paper's editor, Lafayette Young. Initially, the paper was based out of an office on the fifth block of East Walnut. Young's new headquarters, which some called "the most distinguished private structure on the west end of East Locust Street," were located at 134–36 Locust. Being this close to the river, Young argued, he could better serve the two halves of the city. Ultimately, the eastern bank of the Des Moines River was not all that Young had hoped it would be, since Waterbury purchased the plant from Young around 1908 and set to work renovating the property for his own purposes; by the time he was done, the building was almost unrecognizable. Waterbury doubled the size of the plant, and the result was a four-story structure measuring 60 feet wide by 134 feet long.[143]

Just thirty years after opening his company as a young clerk in a drugstore, Waterbury was doing quite well for himself. By 1928, he had laboratories across the country in cities such as New York, New Orleans and Toronto; meanwhile, all of his production and manufacturing was based out of his East Des Moines plant. By this time, Waterbury Chemical Company had grown to the point where it developed and sold twenty-five different products. In 1928, Waterbury's hard work paid off, and he was able to sell the company he had built to St. Louis businessman William R. Warren for $2 million. Warren eventually moved the Waterbury production facility out of Des Moines.[144]

While the sale of the Waterbury Company was certainly a loss for east siders, the business that Waterbury had created laid the groundwork for other chemical manufacturing in East Des Moines. Just before Waterbury sold his company in 1928, a Decorah business, the Meritol Corporation, moved to Des Moines. Initially, it leased the former Colony Building, but after Waterbury left Des Moines, Meritol moved into its former plant. During its time in the former Waterbury plant, Meritol employed anywhere between 100 and 150 people in its plant and kept a sales staff of about 16 to 20 people. Meritol's move to East Des Moines spurred an influx of other chemical and cosmetic manufacturing companies to the city; these included the F.W. Fitch Company, Armand and Chamberlain Medicine. By the 1940s, the building had changed hands again and was now home to J.M. Jamieson's Book Bindery. Sadly, the building was demolished in the later part of the 1960s.[145]

East Des Moines certainly saw a tremendous spike in business and development in the later part of the nineteenth century that then carried into the twentieth century. While some of these ventures failed or were demolished, what came out of this sudden surge of entrepreneurial spirit was the development and organization of a strong class of east side business leaders. As these leaders made their way further into the twentieth century, they expanded their interests beyond purely their own economic interests and began advocating for a larger scale of development in the eastern half of downtown Des Moines.

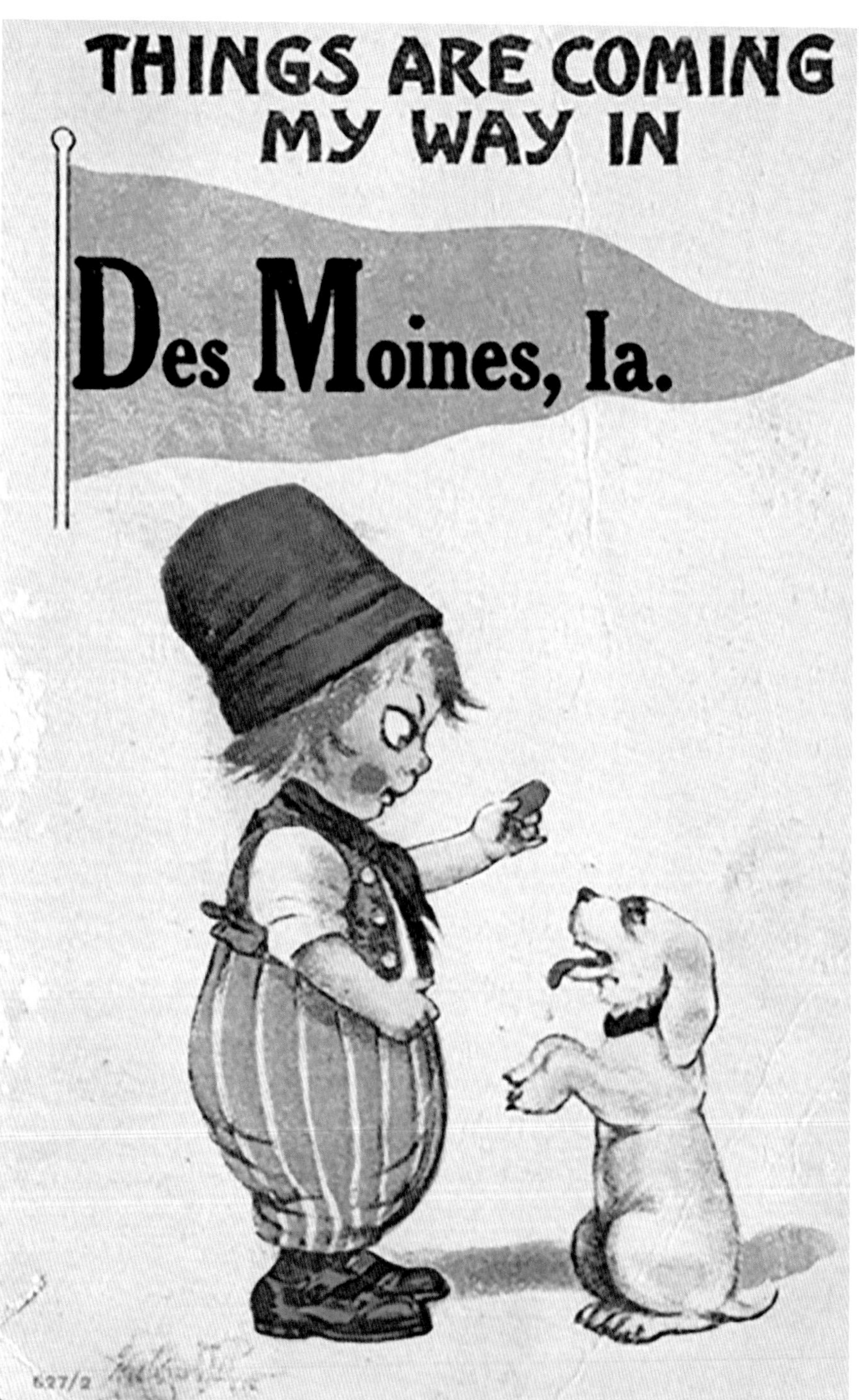

A historic postcard from Des Moines. *DMPL available through a CC-BY License.*

Chapter 6

Civic Engagement in East Des Moines

As Des Moines transitioned into the twentieth century, an air of progress seemed almost palpable throughout the city. Of course, there was all the usual business and industrial progress, but this was something more. Commercial clubs were developing on both sides of the river in order to better serve and represent their respective halves of the city. Efforts were also being made to beautify the city and tidy up what many considered to be the centerpiece of the city, the Des Moines River. And finally, the implementation of a new governing style, aptly named the Des Moines Plan, called for a more active and engaged local government. This chapter will explore the role that East Des Moines played in these new civic efforts to shape the city and, in turn, the ways in which these efforts altered the social and physical landscape of East Des Moines.

The Commercial Club

Moving into the twentieth century, business leaders in East Des Moines determined that it would be in their best interest to establish a more formal organization to better represent them. Calling their group the East Des Moines Commercial Club, their goal was to contribute to "the advancement of East Des Moines and the city at large." Many of these same businessmen were involved in the greater Des Moines Commercial Club, but this new organization aimed to provide more specific attention to East Des Moines businesses, as one member outlined to *Plain Talk* in 1905: "We must look after our interests, because unless we do nobody else will. This is known to every sensible man or at least should be known to him. The formation of a strong, active organization of East Side businessmen is sure to be a great help to the East Side. It is a good work in good hands and brains."[146]

So, on February 25, 1905, the businessmen of East Des Moines gathered at the Capital City State Bank for the inaugural meeting of the East Des Moines Commercial Club. Initially, the club was quite informal, and D.H. Kooker volunteered to serve as the temporary president. Kooker went on to formally serve as the club's first president, with A.B. Elliott serving as vice-president, Addison Parker as secretary and A.C. Miller as the club's treasurer. Nine directors oversaw the club.

In its first year, the East Des Moines Commercial Club outlined a series of specific projects to which its members would devote their time and energy. These projects included building up the downtown area between East Fourth and the river, beautifying the eastern riverfront of the Des Moines River and purchasing more buildings for businesses along the river. Finally, the East Des Moines Commercial Club also made it its goal to strengthen the bonds between the east and west sides of the city and thereby build up a "Greater Des Moines." Just a year after its formation, the East Des Moines Commercial Club had three hundred members. In order to continue stirring up interest among East Des Moines citizens and business owners, the members hosted annual banquets and business meetings that were open to the community.[147]

The East Des Moines Commercial Club not only worked to promote businesses in East Des Moines but also worked to bring more opportunity to its half of the city. In 1907, this meant the Commercial Club lobbied to ensure that the new Coliseum would be constructed on the east side of the Des Moines River.[148] The Coliseum was going to be the premier concert and events venue in downtown Des Moines. The benefits of having this venue located on the east side of the river would have been twofold. First, it would mean greater revenue from concertgoers staying in hotels or eating at restaurants invested in east side businesses, which would certainly benefit east side business owners. Second, recruiting the Coliseum to East Des Moines would help the Commercial Club toward achieving its goal of beautifying the east side of the river and would make the east side a hot spot for tourists visiting the city. East siders were so excited about the prospect of Des Moines' first true "convention center" making its home in East

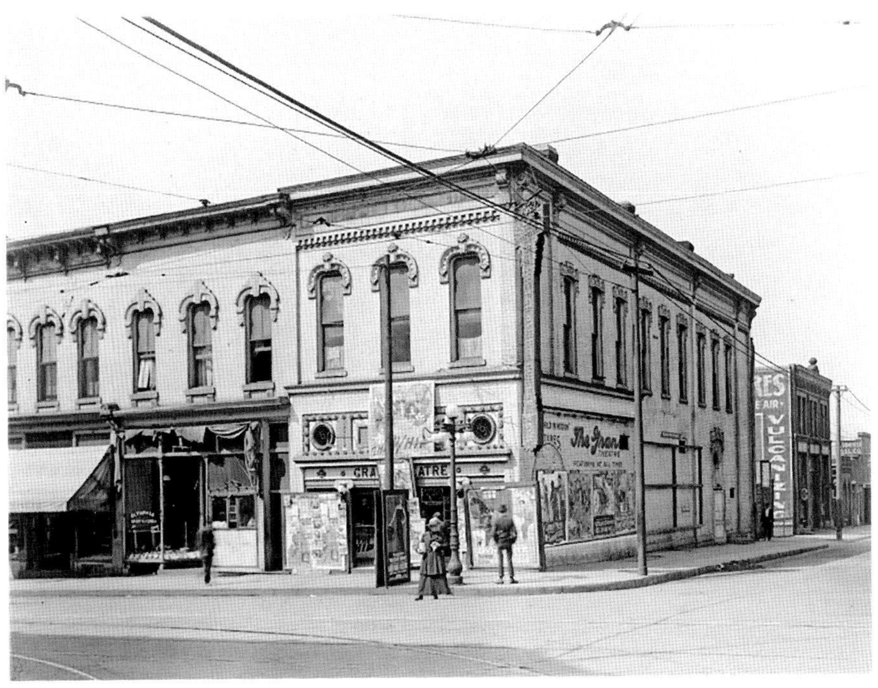

A 1917 photo of the southwest corner of East Sixth and Grand. *DMPL available through a CC-BY License.*

Des Moines that they began proposing scenic park locations for the future Coliseum along the Des Moines River as early as 1905. Unfortunately for the East Des Moines Commercial Club, Frederick Hubbell donated a large tract of land along the western bank of the Des Moines River; Hubbell's donation was accepted, and the Coliseum ultimately made its home in the western half of downtown Des Moines.[149]

While the east siders ultimately did lose out on the Coliseum, they did still have reason to celebrate. In April 1907, the East Side Commercial Club hosted a "monster love and boost feast" in order to celebrate the recent purchase of a riverfront location for the new Municipal Building. Securing the new Municipal Building was a major coup for east siders; *Plain Talk* even went so far as to say that the laying of the cornerstone for the new Municipal Building was "the most important date" in the history of East Des Moines since the cornerstone had been laid at the state capitol in October 1871. While securing the Municipal Building was quite the victory for east siders, it did come with a few consequences; in particular, it increased tensions between East and West Des Moines. The west side of the city also had its own commercial club, and for a time there had been talks of merging the two clubs. But after the east side secured the Municipal Building over the west side, those discussions fell by the wayside.[150]

Later that same year, the East Des Moines Commercial Club continued to pursue the issue of drawing visitors to East Des Moines by turning its attention to the train depots of Des Moines. On October 29, 1907, an anonymous editorial ran in the *Tribune* critiquing the depot situation in East Des Moines. It stated, "One cannot see a visitor or a transient customer once a month, because there is nothing on the East Side to interest him, especially when railway tickets are not sold on the East Side of the river, and the depots are nailed up." The author was certainly justified in his or her frustration. Train tickets were not sold on the east side of the river, so the citizens of East Des Moines had to trek approximately two miles to purchase a ticket.[151] Aside from being a major inconvenience for east siders, this ultimately detracted from east side business. For example, while purchasing tickets at the Union depot on the west side of the river, travelers might be more inclined to do their shopping at nearby businesses, meaning they were less likely to shop on the east side. While the Northwestern line had a depot in East Des Moines, travelers were not able to purchase tickets there, but east siders' primary grievance was with the Union Railroad Company. Every day, there were approximately fifty cars of freight coming and going from the east side. Business leaders felt that this high level of railway traffic merited an east side depot and saw the lack of a Union depot as a direct snub. The idea of a boycott was tossed around but never really amounted to anything. At the Commercial Club's annual Knights of Pythias Hall banquet, two hundred members pledged their support to the issue of east side railway depots.[152]

The depot issue again came to a head in July 1908. By this time, one hundred traveling salesmen had signed a petition stating the need for a depot in downtown East Des Moines. The question of an east side depot was to go before the State Railway Commission when the Rock Island Railway tried to pull one over on everyone. Rock Island abandoned its depot entirely a little over two weeks before the hearing and thereby attempted to claim that the State Railway Commission held no authority over it because there was no functioning depot. Unfortunately for Rock Island, the commission decided that so long as a train stopped in Iowa, a physical depot was not required, but it was the railroad's responsibility to provide the structure for the depot. In the fall of that year, the State Railway Commission changed its tune and ordered the railways with lines running through the state to provide depots. While the Des Moines Union line was willing to comply with the commission's ruling and construct a new depot on the east side, Rock Island refused. In response, the East Side Commercial Club considered seizing the "Market Square" property, whose land had been donated by well-known east sider Alex Scott, and constructing its own depot at this location, but those plans never came to fruition.[153] In 1914, the Commercial Club made it a goal to use the abandoned Rock Island depot as a new location for the Union depot.[154] While the east siders may not have gained the additional depot that they had hoped for, at least the commission had ruled in their favor.

In May 1908, the club was recognized for creating a "business and municipal renaissance" on the east side of the river, and in celebration of this east side renaissance, on October 17 of that year the Commercial Club hosted Bargain Day. This event was meant to celebrate "the opening of a new commercial epoch among the business men of the east side." This "new epoch" was fueled by an east side desire to "compete directly with the west side merchants." In order to do so, east side businessmen were committed to building up "a bigger, busier and greater business district on the east side of the river." Ultimately, Bargain Day was a tremendous success for east side business owners. O'Dea Hardware, a longtime east side business,

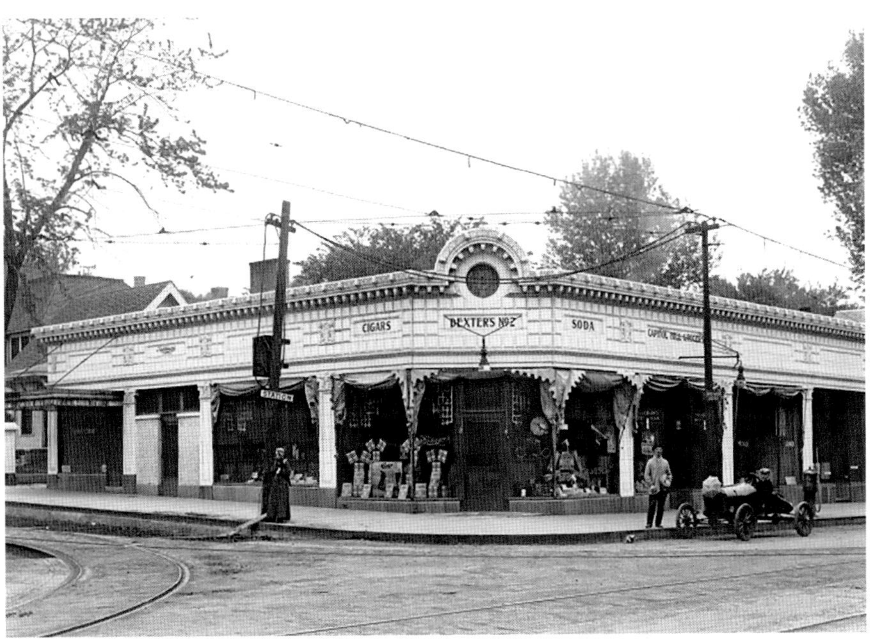

An early photo from East Fourteenth and Grand. *DMPL available through a CC-BY License.*

experienced a 25 percent increase in sales that day. In fact, Bargain Day was so beloved by east siders that it became a weekly event.[155]

The progressive spirit of Bargain Day seemed to be contagious among east siders. Just a few days after the success of Bargain Day, East Des Moines business owners orchestrated a lighting competition in an effort to better light the east side of downtown Des Moines. The competitors included American Lux Lighting Company, the Edison Light Company and the gas company, and the competition resulted in much better lighting throughout East Des Moines, specifically around the Northwestern depot and the Hotel Goldstone. This competition, and the work of the East Des Moines Commercial Club overall, garnered quite a bit of positive press for East Des Moines. One citizen wrote into the *Tribune* stating:

> [The Commercial Club] *has brought East Des Moines into the limelight as a commercial center in a way never before experienced. It has made the downtown thoroughfares of East Des Moines bright and safe at night. It has installed public drinking fountains and has been instrumental in bettering the condition of the streets. It has taken an active interest in building up manufacturing industries. It has secured the promise of improved railroad facilities for East Des Moines.*

The *Tribune* also had the following to say about the East Des Moines Commercial Club: "Never in the history of this portion of the city has there existed such a happy 'community of interests' among the tradesmen as is found today. There is but one slogan for them and that is the up-building and development of East Des Moines."[156]

In 1909, the East Des Moines Commercial Club expressed an interest in more office space on the east side of the river. Ultimately, this interest resulted in the construction of the Teachout Building, which was finished in 1912 and became the second skyscraper on the east side of the river.[157] Later that same year, the Commercial Club began its first attempts at obtaining East Des Moines' first hospital. Club member A.O. Hause led a delegation of east side business owners who met with the Des Moines Homeopathic Board. As an incentive to open a hospital in East Des Moines, Hause and the delegation offered the Des Moines Homeopathic Board $50,000 and a three-acre lot at the corner of East Thirteenth Street and Clark. Ultimately, the club succeeded, and the Des Moines General Hospital made its new home at 603 East Twelfth Street just a few years later.[158]

Over the next several years, the East Des Moines Commercial Club had several other major accomplishments, which it highlighted at its spring banquet in 1911. These accomplishments included enlarging the state fairgrounds, constructing a new East High School, securing riverfront locations for parks, moving the Swedish Lutheran Hospital to East Des Moines and acquiring a passenger depot at the Des Moines Union Railroad. The club also approved plans to enlarge the state capitol grounds and discussed its hopes for enticing an additional railroad to East Des Moines' business district.[159]

The Des Moines Plan

Prior to developing the Des Moines Plan, the city had adopted the Glasgow Plan in 1878. The institution of the Glasgow Plan resulted in a decrease in the number of aldermen throughout the city by half. This plan favored a smaller, more "responsible" governing party over a larger and potentially more "irresponsible" group. Prior to the implementation of the Glasgow Plan, Des Moines struggled to keep pace with the older and more established cities on the eastern border of the state. Under the Glasgow Plan, the city was able to establish a municipal waterworks program, create an industrial improvement association and recruit six railroads to the city. With all these changes, Des Moines was finally able to outpace the cities in the eastern half of the state by 1881.[160]

Transitioning into the twentieth century, the citizens of Des Moines were ready for a new form of government. In 1906, William H. Baily, James G. Berry and John Read were appointed to a 3-man committee tasked with developing a new form of government for the city. They based their new plan on the 1894 Galveston Plan and focused this new form of government with more of a business-model mindset; the draft that they presented to the general assembly proposed that the city council would work together as a municipal board of directors. The draft received the approval and backing of the East Des Moines Commercial Club, and a finalized version was drafted by prominent east sider Archibald L. Stewart. In order to enact the new Des Moines Plan, a committee of 320 men gathered to draft legislation that would allow cities of the first class to make any changes as they saw fit. The bill was passed into law in March 1907. As a result, in June of that same year, a referendum was put forward and approved that called for the implementation of the recently developed Des Moines Plan and allocated $350,000 for the construction of a new Municipal Building.[161] Unfortunately, the passing of the Des Moines Plan was almost derailed by the ongoing rivalry between East and West Des Moines. On the morning the vote was to take place, the *Tribune* newspaper ran the following headline: "East Side Is Attacked by the Plan." Citizens from West Des Moines had apparently been posting signage all over the city calling for voters to vote down the Municipal Building issue. Rumor had it that East Des Moines was the frontrunner for the new Municipal Building, and the *Tribune* posited that West Des Moines feared losing its "monarchical" hold on the city. In response to West Des Moines' smear campaign, east siders were strongly encouraged to get out and vote to save the Municipal Building. Thankfully, East Des Moines came through with the votes and saved the building; historians have referenced this vote as the first east side effort in support of the river beautification movement.[162]

While the Des Moines Plan was meant to streamline local government and enact a business-like structure, citizens of Des Moines were also sold on the fact that this new plan would promote a more accountable form of city government. One of the first steps the city took in being more accountable to the community was to put its support behind the new river beautification project. Additionally, the Des Moines Plan is also credited with supporting Police Commissioner John L. Hamery in his effort to clean up the east side red-light district.[163]

CLEANING UP THE RIVER

As Des Moines settled into the twentieth century, there was increased interest among the citizens of Des Moines in reorganizing the layout of the city, primarily moving toward the river. In 1896, the county board of supervisors had toyed with the idea of relocating the county courthouse to a riverfront location. While a riverfront courthouse never came to fruition, these discussions were the first of many that would focus on framing the Des Moines River, arguably the centerpiece of the city, with the most important buildings in Des Moines.

In order to move to the river, something first had to be done about its current condition. As *Plain Talk* noted in March 1910:

> *There has been a criticism or two lately, in regard to the old shacks of buildings which adorn Walnut, Locust and Court avenue near the river. The public generally are condemning these squatty little houses occupied very largely as residences, or small stores. It must be acknowledged that in a measure they injure the appearance of these streets. It must be remembered too, that this location was once on very low ground and the property owners were not inclined to build any very substantial buildings.*[164]

Prior to the twentieth century, the east and west banks of the Des Moines River were described as "the backsides of two separate cites, each with its commercial, social, and political orientation [which is to say, away from the river], operating in keen rivalry." That being said, it was not necessarily true that either East or West Des Moines had a tidy riverfront. In West Des Moines, the Interurban depot yards, the power plant and the city dump at the connection of the Raccoon and Des Moines Rivers all contributed to a less than pleasant western riverbank. In contrast, while the eastern bank of the Des Moines River had less industrial waste streaming into the river, it appeared to be an east side dumping ground. The banks were covered with overgrown and junk-filled thickets with large billboards rising above the masses of weeds and

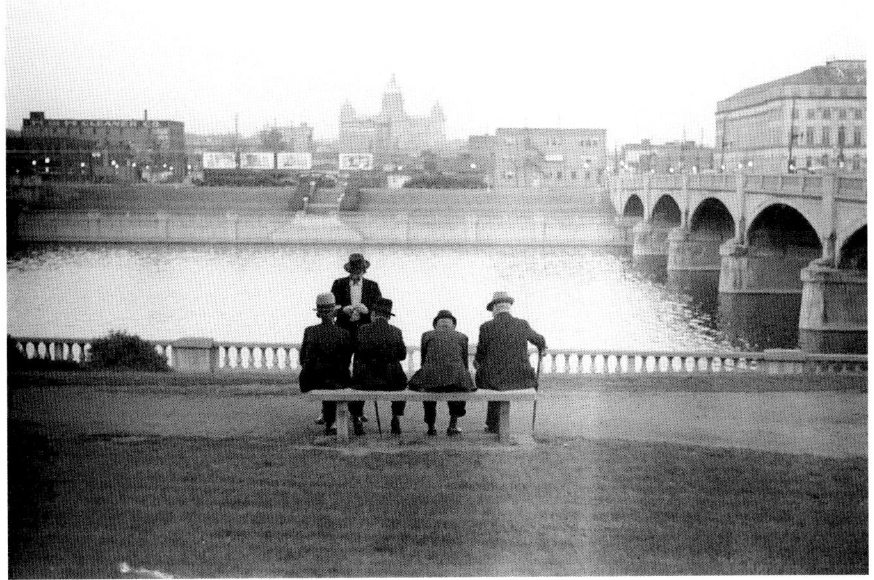

A view of East Des Moines; note the billboards moved back from the riverbank. *Library of Congress, Prints & Photographs Division, FSA/OWI Collection LC-DIG-fsa-8a06253.*

trash. Meanwhile, these two different but equally run-down riverfronts were connected by "rickety old-time bridges."[165]

The solution to this shoddy riverfront was the City Beautiful Movement, which worked to slowly but surely reshape the downtown core throughout the early part of the twentieth century. In order to lay the groundwork for the City Beautiful Movement, two primary changes had to occur within local government, the first of which was the institution of a board of parks commissioner for the city. The second event was the settlement of an 1892 lawsuit that ultimately gave the city jurisdiction over the river and its banks. Both of these events gave the city the authority it needed in order to begin overhauling the riverfront. Aside from cleaning up the river, the City Beautiful Movement also helped to build up the city parks, develop a boulevard system for the city and beautify the grounds of Capitol Hill.[166]

In 1902, the park board stepped in and took control of the riverfront. In planning out the construction along the river, the city had intentionally set the buildings farther back from the river in order to leave room for more landscaping and public space. On both sides of the river, the city included fully landscaped walkways along the edge of the Des Moines River. In order to help protect all of the hard work that went into developing the riverfront from annual flooding, the city also added a dam below the railroad bridges to help maintain water levels.[167] These changes did not go unnoticed by the citizens of Des Moines, as noted by *Plain Talk* in 1910: "Gradually the low grounds are being filled up and now immune from high water. When the riverfront is improved as it will be some of these days and the levees built up to the proper height these grounds will be available for four, six or eight story buildings, at the pleasure of the owners."[168]

Plain Talk certainly had high hopes for the Des Moines Riverfront and hoped that these improvements would set the city on the same trajectory as other great midwestern cities:

> *Any one who is familiar with the location of the Chicago of fifty years ago will tell you that it was reclaimed from a bog and was about as unpromising* [a] *place to build a city as any in the United States. Energy, pluck and spirit will accomplish anything upon which men have set their hearts and concentrated their energies. Had the same feelings existed between the two sides of the river fifty years ago that is existing now the city would be built up solid with good and substantial buildings from capitol to river and the East Des Moines bottoms would have been brought to the same grade as the west side and would have snuggled up to each other as it is doing now*

under a different spirit and with the single idea of making Des Moines the "Chicago of the west."[169]

One of the first major architectural improvements to be made to the riverfront was the Carnegie Library. Initially, the city had considered moving the new library to the former site of the state arsenal, but the Des Moines Women's Club worried that this location was in a flood zone and disliked that it was too far from the residential areas of the city. It wasn't until the state sold a plot of riverfront land in order to purchase the site for the new State Historical Building on East Grand Avenue, just north of the state capitol building, that the city was able to acquire an ideal lot for the new library. The city determined that this lot was a better fit than the old arsenal site, and the library made its new home on the river at West Walnut Street. This was quite the loss for the east side of Des Moines, which had made a valiant effort to recruit the library to its side of the city. Before the turn of the century, prominent east sider Lafayette Young assembled a group of twenty-five east side representatives who offered up the Gilcrest property for the new library. The city clearly passed on this location but kept it in mind for later use.[170]

Aside from landscaping the riverfront, the city also made significant changes to the existing architecture that would be framing the new heart of

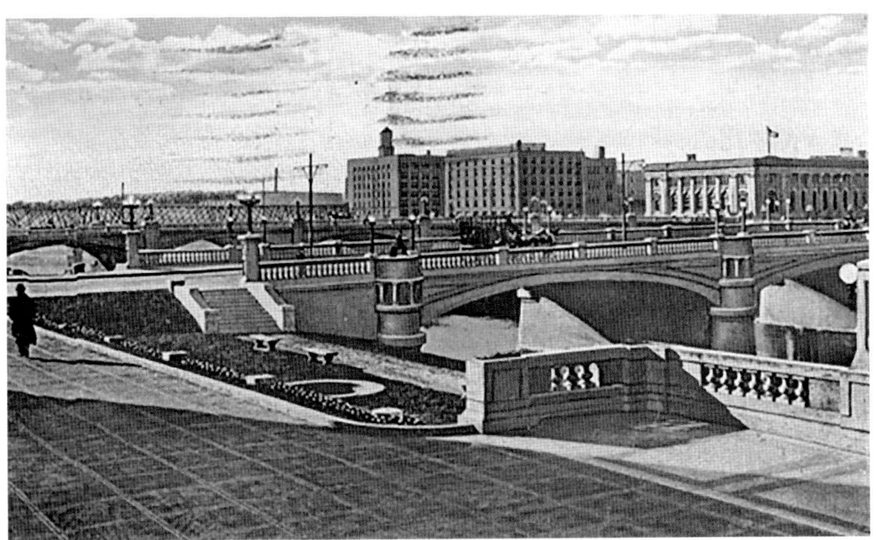

A historic postcard highlighting the reshaping of the riverfront. *DMPL available through a CC-BY License.*

downtown. After the construction of the Coliseum, city leaders turned their attention to cleaning up the neighborhoods around these new gems on the Des Moines Riverfront. On the east side, the focus turned to repaving and elevating streets and removing "riverbank eyesores." This movement against the riverbank eyesores began in June 1909, when the city determined it was necessary to remove privately owned buildings, as they intruded on what was now public property. Some of the first private structures to go were the buildings located between Walnut Street and Court Avenue on the riverfront just across the river from the new library. The city government purchased the buildings, demolished them and cleared the property. In place of the buildings, the city added eight hundred feet of retaining wall. While this retaining wall likely served a very important functional purpose, it was also said that it led to an "improved appearance of the East Side river frontage."[171]

As the city continued to move forward with building up the riverfront, various other groups took an interest and wanted a part in reshaping the heart of downtown Des Moines. Architect Charles Eastman initially developed a design for the new riverfront, but his design was not the only one considered. The Civic Improvement Committee's architect, Frank E. Wetherell, submitted the second design in 1908. Later, the Women's Club also put forward a plan from the city planner, Charles Mulford Robinson. City engineer John Budd submitted a fourth and final plan. Being an engineer, Budd's plan focused more on improvements to the river, such as retaining walls, island removal and channelization, rather than design. Of all the plans submitted, ultimately Wetherell's design was chosen and named the "River Front Civic Center Plan."[172]

The citizens in East Des Moines had been campaigning for the new Municipal Building for many years. In 1906, the East Des Moines Commercial Club went so far as to create a design for the new east side riverfront, with the new Municipal Building, located between Locust and Walnut, as the centerpiece. East Des Moines had housed a Municipal Building since 1875, but this institution was purely to serve the eastern half of Des Moines. The initial East Des Moines Municipal Building was located on the fourth block of East Walnut Street and had only cost $2,500 to construct, but it underwent an $18,000 renovation in 1882.[173] Since this Municipal Building was to serve all of Greater Des Moines, it needed to be far grander. The Municipal Building was the second building, after the library, to begin construction along the Des Moines Riverfront in 1907. Construction along the Des Moines River continued, with work beginning on the post office in 1909 and the Coliseum events center in 1910.[174]

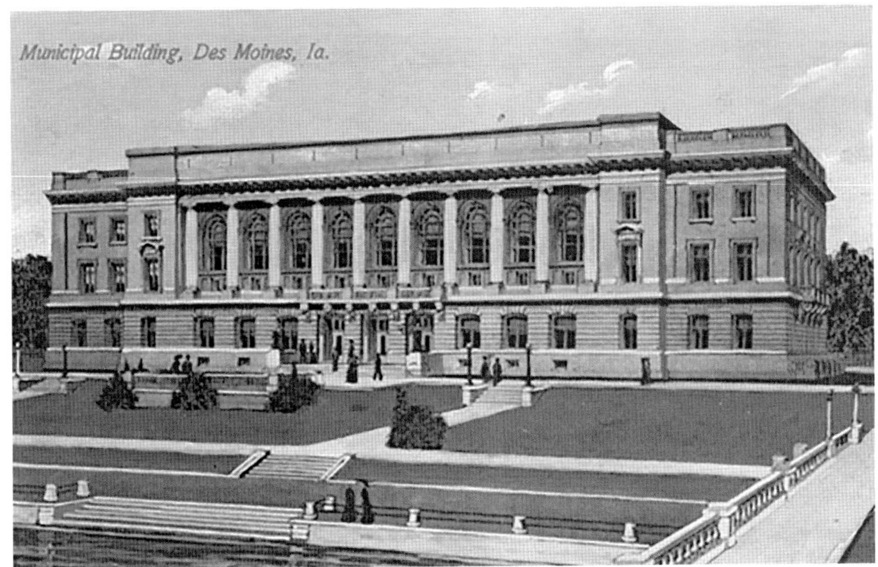

Above: A historic postcard of the Municipal Building. *DMPL available through a CC-BY License.*

Right: Laying the cornerstone of the Municipal Building. *DMPL available through a CC-BY License.*

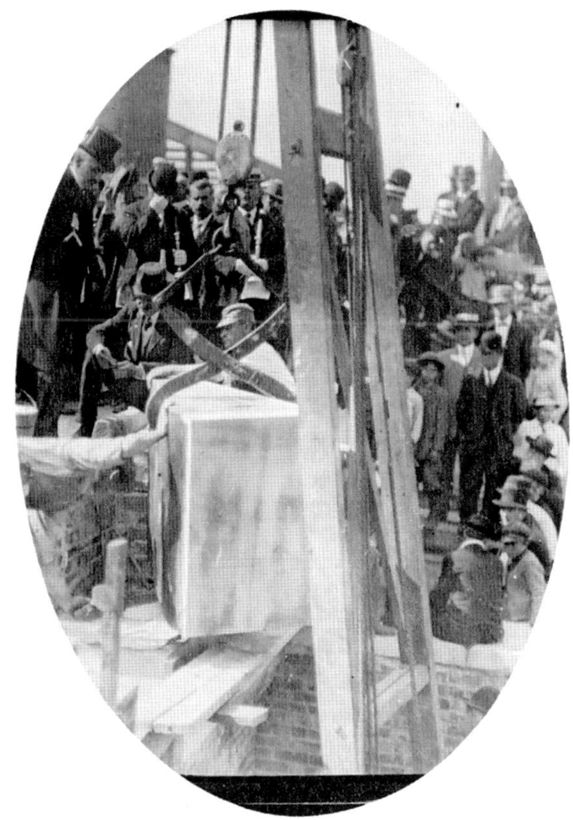

While this move to the river was a citywide effort, in some ways it highlighted the inequity between the eastern and western halves of the city. Early plans for the new Des Moines Riverfront from 1905 outlined the new riverfront developments, all of which at that time were along the western half of the river. For all the worrying that west siders had over losing the Municipal Building, their fears had been for nothing. By 1908, the riverfront plan showed that the west side of the river had gained four new prospective public buildings, including the post office, the new Coliseum and the library, while the east side still only had the Municipal Building.[175]

The east versus west tension reared its ugly head again about a decade later when the city was ready to begin construction on the Municipal Court and the Public Safety Building. In 1916, plans emerged to place the fifth public riverfront structure just south of the Municipal Building on the east side of the river. Construction of this structure came later than the other public buildings on the river and was likely delayed due to the First World War. West siders, primarily the local west side bar association, fought this decision on the grounds that it was inconvenient to have the new municipal court building located so far away from the current county courthouse. Regardless of west side concerns, the Municipal Court and Public Safety Building made their new home along the eastern bank of the Des Moines River, with construction running from 1918 to 1920.[176]

While the city had made great strides to redevelop its downtown core during the first two decades of the twentieth century, the onset of the Great Depression slowed progress. That being said, the city leaders had experienced a tremendous amount of success over the two preceding decades. Through the collaborative efforts of East and West Des Moines, the citizens of Des Moines had adopted a more proactive form of government. The adoption of the Des Moines Plan enabled the city to play a more active and hands-on role in local government. As a result, the city benefited from a more beautiful and publicly accessible riverfront, a boom in construction and development and a series of new and impressive public buildings to frame and highlight the river. While there was a considerable amount of success and progress in this era, that did not necessarily mean the end of old grudges. The East Des Moines Commercial Club certainly made strides to maintain better terms with West Des Moines, but those efforts were in some cases counteracted by competition for riverfront real estate. Ultimately, East Des Moines advocates were successful in gaining several new and beautiful public buildings for their neighborhood.

Conclusion

Had Jerry Gardineer, longtime resident of East Des Moines' old red-light district, spent a day in the Des Moines of the 1970s and 1980s, he would have been quite shocked. Aside from the obvious changes to the landscape, much had changed culturally about Des Moines as a whole. With the growth and development of the towns surrounding Des Moines, as the city moved into the later part of the twentieth century, so did the population of the city. One longtime Des Moines resident recalled that even in the 1940s, while the department stores were full of ladies and sharply dressed men worked in the city selling insurance and whatnot, when the clock struck five o'clock everyone got on the bus and returned to their homes outside Des Moines. The construction of Interstate 235 in 1961 only accelerated the process, and suddenly everyone who worked in the city no longer lived in the city. Instead, they commuted to the surrounding suburbs in West Des Moines, Altoona in the east and Ankeny just north of the city.

About this same time, there was also a shift in consumerism, with the introduction of the first indoor shopping mall and its counterpart, the smaller strip malls. These new shopping centers wanted to be closer to consumers and required a considerable amount of land, which meant they were generally constructed outside the downtown of Des Moines and within the newly established suburbs. While these new shopping malls might have been convenient for suburban consumers, they acted as a death blow to many of the locally owned mom-and-pop shops of East Des Moines. Many longtime locally owned businesses were forced to close their doors. As a

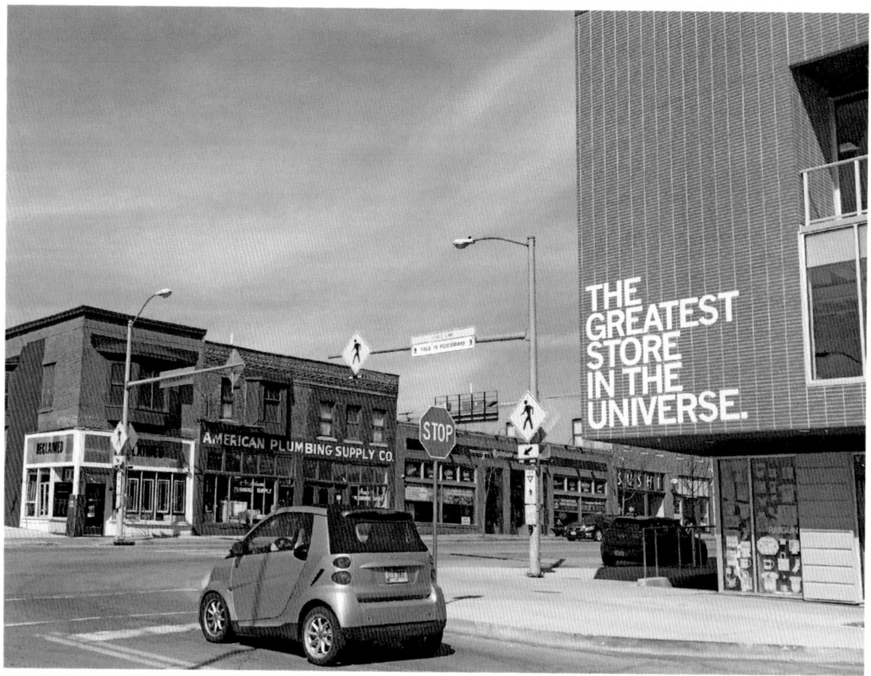

A photo of the East Village today, featuring a blend of new and historic architecture. *Courtesy Hope Mitchell.*

result, the neighborhood began to look rather shabby and run-down, and many buildings that might have been of historical significance to the neighborhood were demolished. Along with the Capital City State Bank Building, which was "finally taken down before it took itself down" in 1981, the east side of the city also saw the demolition of 105 buildings between 1948 and 1989, with 41 buildings demolished between 1980 and 1989 alone.[177]

East side visionary Jim Boyt pinpoints a surprising change that helped to turn the neighborhood around: upgraded sewer systems. Boyt first brought his advertising business to East Des Moines in 1972, when he rented a studio space shared with local photographers and artists for fifty dollars a month. It didn't take long for Boyt to fall for the charm and character of the neighborhood. When the owners of Boyt's rented studio space proposed updating the crumbling brick façade of the building with more modern metal siding, Boyt offered to instead buy the building from them and undertook a restoration of the historic property. Now an east side business owner, Boyt gained a quick introduction to some of the challenges that property owners in East Des Moines faced. One problem in particular was the decrepit sewer system. Due to the run-down sewer system, the basements of properties in the neighborhood were constantly flooding; Boyt realized that it would be hard to incentivize property owners to invest in their properties if they couldn't even keep the basements dry. As a result, Boyt and other east side business owners successfully advocated for an updated sewer system throughout the eastern half of downtown in 1978. From there, Boyt and other east side advocates were able to keep the momentum going and gained buy-in from larger entities, such as the State Historical Society of Iowa, which constructed its downtown Des Moines location on the east side of the river in 1987, and the Embassy Suites hotel, with its riverfront location on the eastern bank of the Des Moines in 1990. It is funny to think that just over one hundred years earlier, prominent east side landowners had united in a similar manner to recruit the new state capitol. While those individuals had sought to ignite business and growth in their half of the city, Boyt and his cohorts looked to reinvigorate the neighborhood those early settlers had created.[178]

As the city moved into the final decade of the twentieth century, it struggled with whether or not to preserve what remained of the eastern half of downtown Des Moines. The city worried that, "having undergone several decades of disinvestment, the East Side currently suffers from negative perceptions. Empty parcels of land, a few boarded-up properties and limited street activity are misinterpreted as inhospitality or lack of safety." In order to fight these perceptions, in 1997 the city aligned with Des Moines Development and received support from the state to form a plan to revive the eastern half of downtown; the result was the Des Moines: Capitol Gateway East Urban Design Plan. As part of the plan, the city worked to improve the landscape throughout the neighborhood—with additional green space, park benches and better lighting to improve safety—and invested in rehabilitating historic properties.

In conjunction with civic efforts to revive the neighborhood, a concerned group of east siders formed with the intent to preserve and promote the historical significance of their neighborhood. Among these concerned citizens was longtime Des Moines architect Kirk Blunck. When Blunck saw the historic neighborhood falling into disrepair, he took the initiative to purchase several east side landmarks, including the Hohberger and Teachout Buildings, and began applying renovations to preserve the historical nature of these structures in the late 1990s. Blunck's efforts helped to jumpstart a movement to rehabilitate the neighborhood, and as the city moved into the twenty-first century, these concerned and proactive citizens organized themselves behind a united effort to revive the neighborhood. In 2002, these citizens formed the Historic East Village, Inc., with the intention of reversing the current trend of demolition and instead encouraging the reuse and rehabilitation of the remaining historical structures in the neighborhood.

All these efforts worked to dramatically reinvigorate the neighborhood; soon, a broad range of businesses moved into the East Village, followed shortly by a vibrant and diverse population, all of whom appreciated the history and character of the Historic East Village. Since the resurgence of the neighborhood in the early 2000s, the Historic East Village has quickly become one of the trendiest places to live, eat and do business. In 2014, the Historic East Village was ranked as one of the top ten "Undercover Stylish Neighborhoods in the U.S." by *Paste Magazine*. Ultimately, everything that has made the Historic East Village a success today is exactly what contributed to the founding of the neighborhood in the first place: a diverse and vibrant population committed to building a thriving and unique neighborhood. While the neighborhood might have experienced a bit of a lull at the turn of the twentieth century, the East Village has certainly come back stronger than ever.[179]

Notes

Introduction

1. *Des Moines Tribune-Capital*, "Gone Is White Chapel."

Chapter 1

2. Dixon, *Centennial History*, 19.
3. Turrill, *Historical Reminiscences*, 10–11; Dixon, *Centennial History*, 15. These two sources differ a bit in their retelling of the events. Turrill claims that Allen only arrived with a small contingent of men and left to retrieve more men and supplies. Dixon's retelling from 1876 makes no mention of Allen's departure, but that does not necessarily mean it did not occur. Since the earlier *Historical Reminiscences* made a point to reference it, I chose to include it in this volume.
4. Turrill, *Historical Reminiscences*, 10–11; Dixon, *Centennial History*, 19–20.
5. Turrill, *Historical Reminiscences*, 11.
6. Ibid., 58–59.
7. Jacobsen, "Lee Township Against the World," 5; Turrill, *Historical Reminiscences*, 12.
8. Dixon, *Centennial History*, 25.
9. Jacobsen, "Lee Township Against the World," 5; Dixon, *Centennial History*, 25; Turrill, *Historical Reminiscences*, 12–13.

10. Dixon, *Centennial History*, 25; Turrill, *Historical Reminiscences*, 16.
11. Dixon, *Centennial History*, 25, Turrill, *Historical Reminiscences*, 17.
12. Dixon, *Centennial History*, 25; Turrill, *Historical Reminiscences*, 17. In *Historical Reminiscences*, Turrill states that the abandoned fort housed newly developed public offices, but he did not specify which public offices were housed in the fort.
13. Turrill, *Historical Reminiscences*, 18–19; Jacobsen, "Lee Township Against the World," 5, 10.
14. Turrill, *Historical Reminiscences*, 19–20.
15. Ibid., 22–23.
16. Ibid., 25.
17. Ibid., 26, 30.
18. Ibid., 57–58.
19. Ibid., 43.
20. Jacobsen, "Lee Township Against the World," 6.
21. Ibid., 5, 10.

Chapter 2

22. Dahl, *Des Moines*, 25.
23. Pratt, *From Cabin to Capital*, 19; Dahl, *Des Moines*, 25.
24. Turrill, *Historical Reminiscences*, 58; Dahl, *Des Moines*, 29, 33.
25. Turrill, *Historical Reminiscences*, 58; Dahl, *Des Moines*, 33–35.
26. Turrill, *Historical Reminiscences*, 58–59.
27. Jacobsen, "Lee Township Against the World," 6; Hammer, *Book of Des Moines*, 63.
28. Porter, *Annals of Polk County*, 174–75, 573; Pratt, *From Cabin to Capital*, 66.
29. Andrews, *Pioneers of Polk County*, 73–77; Brigham, *History of Des Moines*, 174–78.
30. Jacobsen, "Lee Township Against the World," 6–7; Hammer, *Book of Des Moines*, 43, 51; Pratt, *From Cabin to Capital*, 19.
31. Jacobsen, "Lee Township Against the World," 7.
32. Turrill, *Historical Reminiscences*, 85–86.
33. Jacobsen, "Lee Township Against the World," 6–7.
34. Hammer, *Book of Des Moines*, 63.
35. Dahl, *Des Moines*, 35.
36. *Register*, February 27, 1916; Jacobsen, "Lee Township Against the World," 84; Pratt, *From Cabin to Capital*, 20; Andrews, *Pioneers of Polk County*, 96–103.
37. Turrill, *Historical Reminiscences*, 58–59.

38. Jacobsen, "Lee Township Against the World," 8.
39. Pratt, *From Cabin to Capital*, 69.
40. *Register*, April 5, 1995; March 31, 1999; Jacobsen, "Lee Township Against the World," 87; Pratt, *From Cabin to Capital*, 21–22, 71.
41. *Register*, April 5, 1995; March 31, 1999; Jacobsen, "Lee Township Against the World," 87; Pratt, *From Cabin to Capital*, 71.
42. Pratt, *From Cabin to Capital*, 20; *Journal*, September 28, 1875; Jacobsen, "Lee Township Against the World," 21.
43. *Plain Talk*, February 9, March 15, 1884; Jacobsen, "Lee Township Against the World," 45; *Iowa State Register*, February 18, 1882.
44. *Plain Talk*, September 3, 1892; Jacobsen, "Lee Township Against the World," 57; Pratt, *From Cabin to Capital*, 21.
45. *Plain Talk*, March 3, April 14, July 7, August 24, 1894; July 6, 1895; Jacobsen, "Lee Township Against the World," 59, 83; *Register*, February 27, 1916.
46. *Register*, February 27, 1916; June 2, 1999; Jacobsen, "Lee Township Against the World," 83.
47. Pratt, *From Cabin to Capital*, 75; Legislative Information Office, *Iowa State Capitol*, 13, 26.
48. *Plain Talk*, April 26, July 19, August 2, August 16, October 25, 1890; January 3, 1891; Jacobsen, "Lee Township Against the World," 56.
49. *Plain Talk*, March 25, 1905; *Register*, March 31, 1999; Jacobsen, "Lee Township Against the World," 84.
50. Long, "City Beautiful Movement," 13–14.
51. *Register*, February 27, 1916; Jacobsen, "Lee Township Against the World," 83.
52. *Register*, June 25, 1916; Jacobsen, "Lee Township Against the World," 98.
53. Pratt, *From Cabin to Capital*, 79.
54. Ibid., 81–82.
55. Legislative Information Office, *Iowa State Capitol*, 50.

CHAPTER 3

56. *Plain Talk*, February 28, 1885; August 7, 1887; Jacobsen, "Lee Township Against the World," 47.
57. Jacobsen, "Lee Township Against the World," 3.
58. Leslie, *Iowa State Fair*, 31, 38.
59. Playle, *Iowa State Fair*, 7.
60. Ibid.

61. Ibid.; Leslie, *Iowa State Fair*, 47; Shanley, *Our State Fair*, 35.
62. Playle, *Iowa State Fair*, 7; Leslie, *Iowa State Fair*, 47.
63. Leslie, *Iowa State Fair*, 49.
64. Playle, *Iowa State Fair*, 17; Shanley, *Our State Fair*, 35.
65. Leslie, *Iowa State Fair*, 51.
66. Ibid., 49–51; Rasmussen, *Carnival in the Countryside*, 40; *Iowa Farmer* 2 (1854): 162.
67. *Iowa Farmer* 2 (1854): 164–65.
68. Rasmussen, *Carnival in the Countryside*, 41; *Iowa Farmer* 2 (1854): 165.
69. Rasmussen, *Carnival in the Countryside*, 41; *Iowa Farmer* 3 (1855): 47.
70. ISAS *Report* 3 (1856): 15–17; Rasmussen, *Carnival in the Countryside*, 42–43; *Iowa State Register*, September 11, 1880.
71. Rasmussen, *Carnival in the Countryside*, 80–81.
72. Ibid., 80.
73. Ibid., 80–81.
74. Ibid., 81–83.
75. Ibid., 23, 50–51, 54; *Des Moines Register and Leader*, "Constables Make Big Fair Cleanup."
76. Rasmussen, *Carnival in the Countryside*, 50, 55, 68.
77. Ibid., 113–14, 123.
78. Ibid., 11–12; IowaStateFair.org/history; Ta, "Residents Celebrate East Side Night."

CHAPTER 4

79. Dahl, *Des Moines*, 38.
80. *Iowa State Register*, "Libidinous."
81. Ibid., "Arrest of Notorious Cyprians."
82. Richmond, "Passing of Old White Chapel District"; *Des Moines Tribune*, "Whitechapel"; *Des Moines Register and Leader*, "Exodus of Scarlet Women."
83. *State of Iowa v. Mary O'Dell.*
84. *Des Moines Capital*, "Finn's Fists"; *Des Moines News*, "Pounded a Correspondent."
85. *Des Moines News*, "Pounded a Correspondent."
86. Ibid., "They Will Investigate It"; *Des Moines Capital*, "Belvel Indicted"; *Des Moines News*, "Jeanette Allen Comes Back Rich."
87. *Iowa State Register*, "By a Recent Resolution…"; *Iowa State Register*, "It Goes to Mayor Lane."
88. *Des Moines Leader*, "Treasury Is Replenished."

89. Annual Reports of the Sunbeam Mission, 1894–1907.
90. *Des Moines Capital*, "Cramer Hits the Police"; "First Annual Report of Sunbeam Rescue Mission."
91. *Des Moines Leader*, "Treasury Is Replenished"; *Iowa State Register*, "Want to Cleanup East Side Places"; *Des Moines Register and Leader*, "Grand Jury After Owners of Resorts."
92. *Iowa State Register*, "Want to Cleanup East Side Places"; *Des Moines Register and Leader*, "Crusade Against Immoral Section"; *Des Moines Register and Leader*, "Grand Jury After Owners of Resorts."
93. *Des Moines Register and Leader*, "Grand Jury After Owners of Resorts"; *State of Iowa v. W.G. McNulty*; *State of Iowa v. Reese Wilkins*; *State of Iowa v. John Lovich*; *State of Iowa v. John Kime*; *State of Iowa v. Jacob Gottstein.*
94. *Des Moines Register and Leader*, "Red Light People"; *State of Iowa v. T.E. Dowden Company*; *State of Iowa v. J. Gottstein*; *State of Iowa v. Harris Levich.*
95. *State of Iowa v. J. Gottstein*; *State of Iowa v. T.E. Dowden.*
96. *Des Moines Register and Leader*, "Disorderly House."
97. Jacobsen, "Lee Township Against the World," 87.
98. *Des Moines Register and Leader*, "Segregation to Be Considered."
99. Ibid., "Chief Jones Faces Segregation Needs."
100. Ibid., "Grand Jury After Property Owners"; *Des Moines Register and Leader*, "Hamery Proposes New Whitechapel."
101. *Des Moines Tribune-Capital*, "Sees His Face."
102. Jacobsen, "Lee Township Against the World," 87; *Iowa State Register*, "Resorts Deserted."
103. *Des Moines Tribune-Capital*, "Sees His Face"; *Des Moines News*, "White Chapel District"; *Des Moines Tribune-Capital*, "White Chapel Homes Defended"; *Des Moines Register*, "Old White Chapel District."
104. *Des Moines Tribune-Capital*, "Gone Is White Chapel"; Rodgers and Aschbrenner, "New Federal Courthouse."
105. Jacobsen, "Lee Township Against the World," 87.

CHAPTER 5

106. Ibid., 27.
107. *Des Moines Leader*, December 12, 1878; Jacobsen, "Lee Township Against the World," 27.
108. *Des Moines Register*, July 2, 1880; Jacobsen, "Lee Township Against the World," 31.

109. Jacobsen, "Lee Township Against the World," 31.
110. Ibid., 32.
111. *Plain Talk*, October 20, 1883; Jacobsen, "Lee Township Against the World," 40.
112. *Plain Talk*, August 27, 1887; Jacobsen, "Lee Township Against the World," 50.
113. Jacobsen, "Lee Township Against the World," 60.
114. Brigham, *History of Des Moines*, 665–66.
115. Jacobsen, "Lee Township Against the World," 165.
116. Ibid., 116.
117. Ibid., 119.
118. Ibid., 114, 158.
119. Ibid., 115.
120. Bank Minute Book, January 1898; Jacobsen, "Lee Township Against the World," 114.
121. Jacobsen, "Lee Township Against the World," 115, 158; *Plain Talk*, November 17, December 15, 1900.
122. *Des Moines Tribune*, August 26, 1907; and Jacobsen, "Lee Township Against the World," 61.
123. Jacobsen, "Lee Township Against the World," 4, 115, 158.
124. Ibid., 161.
125. Ibid., 128.
126. *Plain Talk*, October 30, 1880; Jacobsen, "Lee Township Against the World," 30.
127. *Des Moines Register*, July 2, 1880; Jacobsen, "Lee Township Against the World," 31.
128. Jacobsen, "Lee Township Against the World," 46.
129. *Des Moines Tribune*, January 5, 1909; January 1, 1910; Jacobsen, "Lee Township Against the World," 90.
130. *Plain Talk*, March 25, 1905; Jacobsen, "Lee Township Against the World," 96.
131. Jacobsen, "Lee Township Against the World," 95–96.
132. Ibid., 96.
133. Ibid.
134. *Plain Talk*, May 13, 1905; Jacobsen, "Lee Township Against the World," 125.
135. Jacobsen, "Lee Township Against the World," 26; *Des Moines Leader*, May 21, July 27, September 29, 1877.
136. Jacobsen, "Lee Township Against the World," 28.

137. *Plain Talk*, February 13, 1892; Jacobsen, "Lee Township Against the World," 28.
138. *Des Moines Register*, October 1, 1881; Jacobsen, "Lee Township Against the World," 33.
139. *Plain Talk*, November 25, 1882; Jacobsen, "Lee Township Against the World," 37.
140. *Plain Talk*, June 6, 1885; Jacobsen, "Lee Township Against the World," 46.
141. Jacobsen, "Lee Township Against the World," 51.
142. *Plain Talk*, February 13, July 23, 1892; March 16, 1895; Jacobsen, "Lee Township Against the World," 57.
143. *Des Moines Tribune*, August 22, 1928; Jacobsen, "Lee Township Against the World," 150–51.
144. *Des Moines Tribune*, August 22, 1928; Jacobsen, "Lee Township Against the World," 101.
145. *Des Moines Tribune*, December 8, 1927; *Des Moines Register*, March 23, 1930; Jacobsen, "Lee Township Against the World," 102, 151.

CHAPTER 6

146. *Plain Talk*, February 25, 1905; Jacobsen, "Lee Township Against the World," 69.
147. Jacobsen, "Lee Township Against the World," 69.
148. *Tribune*, April 12, 1907; Jacobsen, "Lee Township Against the World," 74.
149. *Plain Talk*, April 1, 1905; August 17, 1907; Jacobsen, "Lee Township Against the World," 74.
150. *Plain Talk*, March 31, 1910; Jacobsen, "Lee Township Against the World," 74, 92; *Des Moines Tribune*, April 17, August 29, 1907.
151. *Des Moines Tribune*, October 29, 1907; Jacobsen, "Lee Township Against the World," 75.
152. *Des Moines Tribune*, October 28, November 15, 21, 1907.
153. Ibid., July 5, July 28, September 5, 1908; *Plain Talk*, November 21, 1908; Jacobsen, "Lee Township Against the World," 88.
154. *Des Moines Tribune*, April 22, 1914; Jacobsen, "Lee Township Against the World," 97.
155. Jacobsen, "Lee Township Against the World," 76.
156. Ibid., 77.
157. *Des Moines Tribune*, January 5, 1909; Jacobsen, "Lee Township Against the World," 90.

158. *Des Moines Tribune*, July 29, 1909; *Des Moines Register*, February 13, 2002; Jacobsen, "Lee Township Against the World," 91.
159. Jacobsen, "Lee Township Against the World," 92.
160. Brigham, *History of Des Moines*, 288–92.
161. Ibid., 397–99.
162. *Des Moines Tribune*, June 3, June 24, 1907; Jacobsen, "Lee Township Against the World," 78; Brigham, *History of Des Moines*, 397–99.
163. Jacobsen, "Lee Township Against the World," 80; *Des Moines Register*, August 30, 1908.
164. *Plain Talk*, March 10, 1910; Jacobsen, "Lee Township Against the World," 93.
165. Long, "City Beautiful Movement," 8–11.
166. Ibid., 3–5.
167. *Des Moines Tribune*, June 28, 1908; Jacobsen, "Lee Township Against the World," 79; Long, "City Beautiful Movement," 5–7.
168. *Plain Talk*, March 10, 1910; Jacobsen, "Lee Township Against the World," 93.
169. *Plain Talk*, March 10, 1910; Jacobsen, "Lee Township Against the World," 93.
170. Long, "City Beautiful Movement," 3–5; and Brigham, *History of Des Moines*, 371.
171. *Des Moines Register*, April 12, June 23, 1909; Jacobsen, "Lee Township Against the World," 82.
172. Long, "City Beautiful Movement," 8–11.
173. *Des Moines Leader*, May 4, 1875; *Plain Talk*, September 2, 1882; Jacobsen, "Lee Township Against the World," 27, 36.
174. Long, "City Beautiful Movement," 12.
175. *Des Moines Tribune*, June 28, 1908; Jacobsen, "Lee Township Against the World," 79; Long, "City Beautiful Movement," 5–7.
176. *Des Moines Register*, April 16, 1916; Jacobsen, "Lee Township Against the World," 81; *Des Moines Magazine*, March 1917.

Conclusion

177. Jacobsen, "Lee Township Against the World," 4; Oltrogge, *Images of America: East Village*, introduction.
178. Aschbrenner, "This Man Had a Front Row Seat."
179. Andrews, "10 Undercover Stylish Neighborhoods."

Selected Bibliography

Books

Andrews, Lorenzo F. *Pioneers of Polk County, Iowa and Reminiscences of Early Days*. 2 vols. Des Moines, IA: Baker-Trisler Company, 1908.

Brigham, Johnson. *History of Des Moines and Polk County, Iowa*. 2 vols. Chicago: S.J. Clarke Publishing Company, 1911.

Dahl, Orin L. *Des Moines: Capital City*. Tulsa, OK: Continental Heritage, Inc., 1978.

Dixon, J.M. *Centennial History of Polk County, Iowa*. Des Moines, IA: State Register, 1876.

Hammer, Ilda M. *The Book of Des Moines*. Des Moines, IA: Board of Education, 1947.

Legislative Information Office. *Iowa State Capitol: A Peek into the Past*. Des Moines, IA: Legislative Information Office, 2000.

Leslie, Thomas. *Iowa State Fair: Country Comes to Town*. New York: Princeton Architectural Press, 2007.

Oltrogge, Sarah C. *Images of America: East Village*. Charleston, SC: Arcadia Publishing, 2009.

Playle, Ron. *Iowa State Fair: In Vintage Postcards*. Postcard History Series. Charleston, SC: Arcadia Publishing, 2006.

Porter, Will. *Annals of Polk County and the City of Des Moines*. Des Moines, IA: George A. Miller Printing Company, 1898.

Pratt, LeRoy G. *From Cabin to Capital*. 3rd ed. Des Moines: State of Iowa, Department of Public Instruction, 1974.

Rasmussen, Chris. *Carnival in the Countryside: The History of the Iowa State Fair*. Iowa City: University of Iowa Press, 2015.

Shanley, Mary Kay. *Our State Fair: Iowa's Blue Ribbon Story*. Des Moines: Iowa State Fair Blue Ribbon Foundation, 2000.

Turrill, H.B. *Historical Reminiscences of the City of Des Moines*. N.p., 1857.

Articles and Newspaper Articles

Andrews, Mari. "10 Undercover Stylish Neighborhoods in the US." *Paste Magazine*, 2014. www.pastemagazine.com/blogs/lists/2014/04/10-undercover-stylish-neighborhoods.html.

Aschbrenner, Joe. "This Man Had a Front Row Seat for the East Village Transformation." *Des Moines Register*, April 8, 2016.

Des Moines Capital. "Belvel Indicted." March 7, 1892.

———. "Cramer Hits the Police." February 2, 1898.

———. "Finn's Fists: The Senator from Taylor Knock H.M. Belvel Down." February 19, 1892, 4:00 p.m. edition.

———. "Jeanette Allen Was Arrested Yesterday on the Indictment…" February 26, 1892.

Des Moines Leader. "Treasury Is Replenished." May 1, 1900.

Des Moines News. "Jeanette Allen Comes Back Rich." December 13, 1901.

———. "Pounded a Correspondent." February 20, 1892.

———. "They Will Investigate It: The Senate Will Get to the Bottom of the Alleged Visit to Whitechapel." February 20, 1892.

———. "White Chapel District May Be Condemned." May 27, 1922.

Des Moines Register. "Old White Chapel District Being Leveled." October 30, 1931.

Des Moines Register and Leader. "Chief Jones Faces Segregation Needs: The Disorderly Houses Are Spreading Over the City." July 23, 1906.

———. "Constables Make Big Fair Cleanup." August 26, 1906.

———. "Crusade Against Immoral Section." November 20, 1904.

———. "The Disorderly House." July 27, 1906.

———. "Exodus of Scarlet Women from City." September 2, 1906.

———. "Grand Jury After Owners of Resorts." December 10, 1904.

———. "Grand Jury After Property Owners." June 16, 1906.

———. "Hamery Proposes New Whitechapel." July 24, 1906.

———. "Red Light People Must Move Out." July 21, 1906.

———. "Segregation to Be Considered." December 26, 1904.

Des Moines Tribune. "Whitechapel (Twenty Years Ago Heart of Underworld) Will Soon Fall Under Picks of Wrecking Gang." May 8, 1926.

Des Moines Tribune-Capital. "Gone Is White Chapel District Here but Old Signs Recall 'Glorious' Days." August 21, 1929.

———. "Sees His Face in New Book: Supt. Hamery Reads His Editorial Comments with Surprise." December 15, 1909.

———. "White Chapel Homes Defended in Council." October 18, 1928.

Iowa State Register. "Arrest of Notorious Cyprians." June 27, 1866.

———. "By a Recent Resolution…" December 18, 1880.

———. "It Goes to Mayor Lane." January 5, 1893.

———. "Libidinous." May 29, 1862.

———. "Resorts Deserted; Women Penniless." August 31, 1908.

———. "Want to Cleanup East Side Places." November 19, 1904.

Long, Barbara Beving. "The City Beautiful Movement and City Planning in Des Moines, Iowa, 1982–1938." N.p., 1987.

Richmond, Rider. "Passing of Old White Chapel District Recalls Palmy Days of Late Nineties: Brick Tenements Once Were Hangout for Scarlet Vice." *Des Moines Register*, October 31, 1931.

Rodgers, Grant, and Joel Aschbrenner. "New Federal Courthouse Planned in Des Moines." *Des Moines Register*, December 23, 2015.

Ta, Linh. "Residents Celebrate East Side Night at Iowa State Fair." *Des Moines Register*, August 15, 2015.

REPORTS

Cramer, Frank L. "Eleventh Annual Report of Sunbeam Mission: The Open Door, Des Moines Iowa." Geo A. Miller PTG. Co., Des Moines, January 1, 1904. State Historical Society of Iowa Library. State Archives of Iowa.

———. "First Annual Repot of Sunbeam Rescue Mission of Des Moines, Iowa, 212 Walnut St." Iowa Printing Co., Des Moines, January 1, 1894. State Historical Society of Iowa Library. State Archives of Iowa.

———. "Second Annual Report of Sunbeam Rescue Mission and Door of Hope." Iowa Printing Co., Des Moines, January 1, 1895. State Historical Society of Iowa Library. State Archives of Iowa.

———. "Tenth Annual Report of Sunbeam Mission: The Open Door." Geo A. Miller PTG. Co., Des Moines, January 1, 1903. State Historical Society of Iowa Library. State Archives of Iowa.

———. "Third Annual Report of Sunbeam Rescue Mission and Door of Hope." Iowa Printing Co., Des Moines, January 1, 1896. State Historical Society of Iowa Library. State Archives of Iowa.

———. "Thirteenth Annual Report of Sunbeam Mission: The Open Door, Des Moines, Iowa." Geo A. Miller PTG. Co., Des Moines, January 1, 1906. State Historical Society of Iowa Library. State Archives of Iowa.

Jacobsen, James E. "Lee Township Against the World: The Commercial Architecture and History of Downtown East Des Moines, Iowa 1877–1952." Des Moines, IA: History Pays! Historic Preservation Firm, 2002.

COURT CASES

State of Iowa v. Harris Levich (1907).

State of Iowa v. Jacob Gottstein (1886).

State of Iowa v. J. Gottstein (1907).

State of Iowa v. John Kime (1892).

State of Iowa v. Mary O'Dell (1874).

State of Iowa v. Reese Witkins (1883).

State of Iowa v. T.E. Dowden Company (1907).

State of Iowa v. W.G. McNulty (1883).

Index

D

E

F

G

H

I

J

K

L

About the Author

While studying the history of prostitution in the Midwest and pursuing her MA in history at Iowa State University, Hope Mitchell quickly fell in love with the history of Des Moines. Her thesis, "Sacrificing Our Daughters: Changing Perceptions of Prostitution in Iowa, 1880–1915," was the 2014 winner of the Iowa History Center's Outstanding Master's Thesis Award. Currently, Hope is the assistant coordinator of the Iowa State University Digital Repository at Parks Library, but she spends her free time tracing the history of Iowa's red-light districts and disreputable women.